Denim
mania

ALSO BY
SISTAHS OF HARLEM
Carmen Webber and
. . Carmia Marshall . .

T-Shirt Makeovers:
20 Transformations for Fabulous Fashions

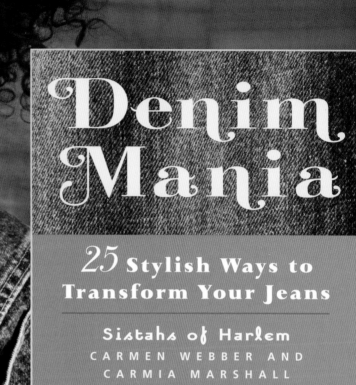

Denim Mania

25 Stylish Ways to Transform Your Jeans

Sistahs of Harlem

**CARMEN WEBBER AND
CARMIA MARSHALL**

ST. MARTIN'S GRIFFIN

NEW YORK

PHOTOGRAPHS BY DERRICK GOMEZ
ILLUSTRATIONS BY CARMEN WEBBER
STYLING BY CARMIA MARSHALL
BOOK DESIGN BY DEBORAH KERNER

www.stmartins.com

Library of Congress Cataloging-in-Publication Data

Webber, Carmen.
    Denim mania : 25 stylish ways to
    transform your jeans / Carmen
    Webber and Carmia Marshall.—
    1st ed.
        p. cm.
    Includes index.
ISBN-13: 978-0-312-35991-1
ISBN-10: 0-312-35991-8
1. Jeans (Clothing). 2. Clothing and
    dress—Remaking. 3. Title. I. Title.

TT605 . W42 2008
687'.1—dc22

First Edition: March 2008
10 9 8 7 6 5 4 3 2 1

contents

acknowledgments

Thank you's:

Thank you, God, for giving us the wisdom and the strength to move forward. **Betty Marshall, my mother.** Without you, I would not exist. I cannot imagine my life without you. You are pure sunshine. I love you! **Takiyah Jackson,** the perfect sister! My voice of reason. I love you! **Frederick Jackson,** I'm proud that you are my brother-in-law! I love you! **Sandra Marshall.** You're completely amazing. You helped me to pursue my dreams! I love you. Thanks for your constant support. To the entire **Jones and Marshall family and friends,** thanks for believing! **Libbie Johnson,** my dearest mother, you truly are that gust of wind that I soar above. Thank you so very much for your continual love and support for Sistahs of Harlem and all that we do, and that I do. These amazing books sprang from the great experiences I have had coming into the world through you. I truly appreciate you. I love you. **Cherod and Maurice Webber,** you two have truly been the backbone of helping me through the blood, sweat, and tears of bringing this book to life. I love you both. **Winston Webber,** thank you for exposing me to Picasso at such a young age. It has surely paid off. **Mama Faye Webber,** you truly are remarkable in your shared life experiences. Thank you so very much for those trips to the cotton fields. What a treat to have such amazing memories. I love you, and appreciate your support! **Daddy Jerry (Jerry Johnson),** thanks to the the world's coolest dad! I appreciate your walk through memory lane on the denim research for this book. I love you. **Auntie Eb (Evelyn Matthews),** I never would have had the courage to cut, slice, embellish, patch up, and paint my jeans without exposure to your amazing denim style! Thanks for nurturing my artistic vision!! **Grandma Fannie,** thanks to you for being that grand diva all of those years. Your smashing denim suits left a fantastic impression. I appreciate your encouragement. I love you! **Nancy and Francis Webber,** you two truly always embraced that artist that I am. I love you both. Thanks. **Simone Thomas Webber,** thanks so much for all of your support through this project. It was fantastic wearing matching denim culottes handmade by Mama Faye at the age of six, remember? Love you! **Samiyah Johnson,** my nonbiological sister, and amazing friend for more than a decade! Thanks for all your hard work. **Jackie Stone,** a wordsmith! An amazing friendship. Thanks for your support. **Carmencita Whonder,** a remarkable spirit and topnotch friend, thanks for ten years of friendship! Your honesty, advice, nonjudgment, and support are a great asset to my life. **Marta Hallett,** thank you so much! *T-Shirt Makeovers* has opened so many doors! **Martha Moran,** a lifesaver! Your knowledge helped to make this book flawless. **Adrienne Ingrum,** the best agent in the universe—the rock star of agents! Look forward to a lifelong relationship! **BJ Berti,** thank you for the opportunity to share our ideas with the world. **Erica Sewell and Jasaun Buckner,** you are wonderful friends and immense talents. I'm glad that you are a part of my life. Thank you! **Fatima Robinson, Mary Gehlhar, and Kendall Farr,** thanks for your continued support. **Derrick Gomez,** dynamic photographer. You did it again. The images are wonderful. **Reneé Rupcich,** supreme retoucher. Thank you! **Leonard Robinson, Zakiaayah Salim, and Princess Mhoon–Cooper,** die-hard Sistah's fans and amazing friends. Your support is appreciated and won't be forgotten. **Sony Heron,** Luna Llena Management rocks! Thanks! **David Yoon,** your graphic design is amazing. **Kimberley Britto-Ukkerd,** Kimiwear bracelets rock! Thanks for being a great friend! I love you! **Josama,** thanks for being there. I love you! **Dana Gibbs and Shade Boyewa,** thanks for your vanity skills. **Jasmine Faustino,** thanks for your patience! **Worie Vice,** Style King! Thanks for your support. **Katrina and Natalie Markoff,** thank you so very much for all of your sweetness. You are the best mentors ever! Vosges Chocolates rocks! **Nicci Hall,** thanks for your support! **Phyllis Magidson,** thanks for loving Sistahs of Harlem. **Cherisse Bradley,** beautiful, soulful woman! I love you. Thanks for always being there. **Ali and Frances Bradley,** my little sisters, I love yall! **Audrey Dussard,** the best accountant in the world. We appreciate you. **Mariel Keio, Amanda, Amy, Nekesha, and Amber,** you look beautiful in the photos. **Nichelle Sanders,** thank you for your patience, guidance, and witty ideas! **Dale from Pure Accessories Show Room NYC,** thank you for supporting the Sistahs of Harlem vision. **Joseph Burton,** thanks for always being in me. I adore you, too! **Connis Cabbs,** thanks for all of the wisdom, big sistah! **Joselyn Harmon,** you're the true whimsical denim diva. Thanks for your support. **N' Dea Davenport,** to the world's one and only fabulous rock star!!! Thanks for all of your support! **Michelle and Ben Bagby,** thank you so very much for the brilliance. **Valarie Peters,** you are a true, dear friend. Thanks for the support and love during this project!!! Love you. **For all of the friends and family who we forgot, please blame the mind and not the heart.**

introduction

Carmen: I grew up in the South, and the history of cotton and denim was an integral part of my childhood experience. I learned the importance of fabric mills and cotton plantations at a young age. I vividly remember Mama Faye, my grandmother, loading my cousins and me into her shiny, navy blue Monte Carlo and driving us along small winding back roads in Kings Mountain, North Carolina, to visit the cotton fields. She explained to us the importance of cotton and encouraged us to go grab a branch with a nice fluffy white cotton bud on it. At that time, the history lesson was not that interesting; however, the cotton actually growing out of a thorny branch was fascinating to us.

In the South, denim was practically the uniform for blue-collar workers and the knock-around gear for white-collar workers. My grandfather Esper Webber, whom I call Pawpaw, and my great-grandmother Mama Lily were carefree souls. Mama Lily and my great-grandfather Bruce Whitworth spent a lot of time in their jeans while gardening and tending a small family farm in their spare time. I used to own a pair of Levi's coveralls that belonged to Daddy Bruce. They took me from the late 1980s well into the early 1990s.

My fondest memories are of my mother's sister Aunt Evelyn (known as Auntie Eb to this day because, as toddlers, we could not pronounce Evelyn and would say Eb), who sported a fabulous eight-inch afro and really cool T-shirts and wore jeans in all different styles. My favorite was the pair she had completely transformed by covering the entire surface with cool patches. She would sometimes hop into her sporty MG convertible with black leather seats and drive from Lexington to Charlotte to help me decorate my jeans. She was the youngest of the seven children in my mother's family and was in her late teens in the '70s. She wore denim every way imaginable.

My first experiences with denim jeans, knockarounds, dungarees, whatever you chose to call the famous raw cotton garment, spawned the love affair that I have with denim today. No matter what the makeup of my wardrobe, I will always come back to denim.

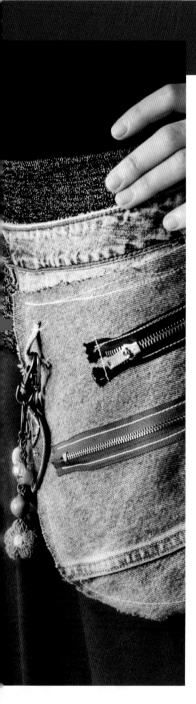

Carmia: I cannot imagine my life without denim. From my

toddler years in OshKosh B'Gosh denim overalls with pink ruffled trim to today's slinky, eye-catching indigo Japanese denim with Lycra (it has to fit the booty)—wearing denim makes me feel matchless. I can always depend on my denim to complete a look. I can re-create every look in my jeans—fiery, bohemian, funky, spunky, preppy, cool, and classic. My blues can accelerate from chilling to kicking it hard in the streets. Like fine wine and confident women (as my mother would say), denim doesn't covet cosmetic surgery; it ages without remorse and feels especially good on the body when doing so.

Every brand brings something different to the table. You can own five pairs of boot-cut jeans—all extremely different. The finishes may vary from indigo blue to flaming red, some beautifully torn, or distressed with random abrasions, whiskers, and rips that hang poetically from the jean; others cool, clean, and simple. Embell-ishments add bling; even the style of the pockets can completely change the feeling of the jean.

Denim is in demand for all forms of apparel. We're singing entire songs—not just a verse—about them. My jeans, as the Black Eyed Peas song says, "showcase my lovely lady lumps!" My jean jacket glides over any style shirt: baby doll, baby tees, long- and short-sleeved button-downs. I can throw a denim jacket over a little black dress and still look remarkable. I can carry a denim clutch with a beaded gown and, yes, it's appropriate!

I will never forget the time when I was rushing to Henri Bendel's before it closed and I managed to snag the sleeve of my vintage denim jacket on a nail of a scaffold. I was livid. I had just purchased it from a local Salvation Army store. Not once did I consider throwing it away. I took my jacket home, cut off the sleeves, and used the scraps to make a flower as an additional detail. I also jazzed it up with some leather scraps used as appliqués. The snag metamorphosed into one fine-looking vest.

I own more than twenty pairs of jeans. I have old-school bells, high-waisted Levi's, cigarettes, boot cut, wide, beaded, straight leg, and more, yet I have to stop myself from buying even more. They rock the body in the right places. Denim is powerful. Denim is spicy. Denim is the most utilized and reliable material in my closet.

The Sistahs of Harlem Philosophy

Since the inception of the Sistahs of Harlem, we have been known for our deconstructed pieces—for our ability to take existing pieces of clothing and to transform them into new, magical, one-of-a-kind pieces. We like to refer to our clothing as "street couture." This is our approach to all projects in this book as well. Each garment was created as if we were designing a seasonal collection and with the same asthetic as our custom collections. We want you to feel as stylish, unique, and confident in the clothing and accessories that you make as in the ones you purchase.

Some of the projects in the book require little or no sewing experience. Others require some sewing experience and a sewing machine. We're confident that you can do it. Enjoy and happy sewing!

Carmen D. Webber

Carmia Marshall

S i s t a h s   o f   H a r l e m

JEANS

denimwise

A Brief History of Denim

Denim is defined as a coarse, durable, twill-weave cotton fabric. The first denim came from a French fabric of silk and wool. Made in Nîmes, it was called *serge de Nîmes*. Jeans originated in Genoa, Italy, when the city was an independent republic and a naval power. The Genoese navy required all-purpose trousers for its sailors that could be worn wet or dry and with legs that could easily be rolled up to wear while swabbing the deck. Jeans were laundered by dragging them in large mesh nets behind the ship, and the seawater would bleach them. It is possible the French term *bleu de Gênes*, from the Italian *blu di Genoa* (blue of Genoa), referring to the dye of their fabric, is the origin of term the *blue jean*. Today jean, blue jean, and denim are nearly synonymous.

The prototype of the American-made work trouser was made originally with a cream-colored cotton duck fabric. As the cream color did not, however, disguise the soil and filth from the normal workday, an indigo-colored denim was introduced to camouflage the unwanted grime. The durability of indigo as a color and its darkness of tone made the best choice. The Amoskeag Manufacturing Company in Manchester, New Hampshire, was one of the first mills to make a blue denim fabric, in the late 1800s, using a dye made from fermenting the leaves of the indigo plant. It was a time-consuming process, requiring an overwhelming amount of labor. Synthetic indigo was later developed in the laboratory to create the same color as the blue-pro-ducing plant.

Today everyone wears denim—from the superstars of Hollywood to the sanitation engineers of New York City. Denim is well cultured and exposed to myriad lifestyles. It's nonjudgmental and effortlessly maneuvers from the poorest to the most luxurious atmosphere. Denim, at some point of its existence, has represented the working, the rebellious, the young, the old, the intellectuals, the artists, and the free.

Denim's versatility is amazing. Denim is ingrained in American culture. To dis-regard its impact on the glitzy, fickle, and ever-changing world of fashion would be simply silly. The role of denim is profound. It is the "rebel fabric," the fabric of the working class, the fabric that endures wear and tear gracefully without noticeable damage, the fabric of freedom and self-expression. Overrated? We think not!

Million-Dollar Jeans

Eyes bulged and jaws dropped in the tents of Bryant Park during Fashion Week, as Jennifer Lopez unveiled the Diamond Jean. This pair of signature jeans made from Turkish denim, and hand washed in L.A. held a 17-carat, D-color diamond-encrusted button, flanked by nine 33-point stones around the pockets and waist. Priced at $2 million, this is the most extravagant jean ever produced.

Shades of Denim

Denim comes in so many shades of blue, it is almost impossible to create a universal color chart, since the colors of denim change from brand to brand. From our observations on the street, we've determined that the darker the denim, the more dressy the feel. The lighter shades of blue are more casual. But, the more casual blues can be upgraded to a more elegant look by pairing them with an upscale button-front blouse, beaded tunic, or tailored blazer with silk camisole.

Here's our basic color primer with our take on how to wear denim for maximum impact:

DARK MIDNIGHT BLUE: Almost black, in this color you're moving in and out of swank environments. In fact, people have to look twice to realize that you're wearing blue jeans. The midnight blue is great for upscale casual; it's very urbane.

INDIGO BLUE: This is the basic, and prime, jean color. Simple, unadorned, plain-finished indigo blue is the classic color for denim jeans. A dark, rich blue that moves from day to night, this color is extremely versatile as well as the most popular. You can wear it anyway you want—dress it up with a special blouse or jacket, or play it down and basic with a T-shirt or zip-front sweatshirt. It all depends on your place of action!

TRUE MEDIUM BLUE: Can move from day to night; this is a good transitional color

PALE LIGHT BLUE: Usually worn during the day; it's light and refreshing

ALMOST WHITE: Very pale blue, almost white, this is a great color for the beach. It's extremely light, airy, and fresh. It is a surprisingly good night color during the warmer months of the year, and a great color to wear during the day.

WHITE: White jeans, worn with an upscale top, are a class act.

OTHER COLORS: Denim comes in every color imaginable—kelly green, eggplant, charcoal, red, copper, white, black, rust, Bordeaux—the colors available are limitless. These colors are fun to wear and are especially good for casual environments.

Glossary of Denim Styles

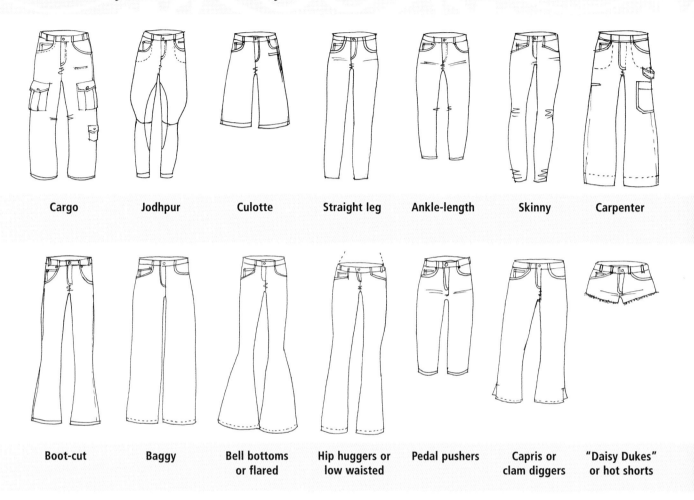

Cargo   Jodhpur   Culotte   Straight leg   Ankle-length   Skinny   Carpenter

Boot-cut   Baggy   Bell bottoms or flared   Hip huggers or low waisted   Pedal pushers   Capris or clam diggers   "Daisy Dukes" or hot shorts

Denim Washes

You can create an aged appearance or enhance the softness of denim by washing it. There are different ways to wash denim, each producing a different final color and fabric finish. The technology used for various washes is taking the humble blue jean to a new plateau of sophistication. By the time you read this book, more first-class innovative washes will, of course, be on the market. A new denim trend will be sweeping the racks of stores near you.

ACID WASH: A method of soaking pumice stones in bleach and then adding them to a dryer full of denim to create "random" bleach spots

DIRTY ANTIQUE WASH: The fabric has been softened, shrunk, and faded, and excess dye has been removed, creating controlled fading in some areas, such as on the thighs and rear. Irregular appearance looks homespun, worn, and gracefully aged.

STONEWASH: Stones are used to create abrasions, whiskers, chevrons, or other damage marks on parts of the garment and the seams.

Other Denim Finishes

Washing is not the only way to change the look and feel of denim fabric. Abrasion, dyeing, cutting, and bleaching can also make denim look well aged and give it a softer hand.

INDIGO BLUE: Once harvested from plants, indigo dye is now generally synthesized from chemicals. But pure, genuine indigo can produce deep brilliant blues that cannot be duplicated with any other dye.

OVERDYEING: The garment or fabric is re-dyed with another color, one color layered over another. Most frequently used on indigo or black denim fabric, which is overdyed with black.

RIPPED AND TORN: An aging process involving fabric abrasion, where the denim is actually shredded and torn

HAND SANDING: A way of reproducing such patterns as whiskers, chevrons, or other damage marks in localized areas, simulating long-term wear

SANDBLASTING: Jeans are sprayed with sand by hand in specific areas before washing to create a used look in those areas.

SUN BLEACHING: A combination of sandblasting and bleach gives the denim a very soft and powdery feel.

Types of Denim

Known for its sturdy twill weave, denim is a genius fabric. The weave contributes its strength. The blue/indigo yarns are the lengthwise or *warp* (parallel to the selvage). The white yarns run across the fabric width (the *weft* threads). Denim is traditionally woven with 100 percent cotton fiber, but today it is often blended with Lycra (for stretch) and polyester (to prevent shrinkage) and other materials to manipulate the life span of the eternal fabric.

Understanding the weave and blends requires some studying. Grab a pair of jeans and just look at them. The terms will start to make sense. Touch your jeans. Experience the *hand* (the feel of denim—from soft to coarse) of your denim as you determine what works best for you. Here is a simple summary of the most popular denim blends used today.

Organic Denim
These babies are all nat-u-ral!

No pesticides or other artificial chemicals are applied in the farming of the cotton that is used to produce the denim. For the fashion and ecology savvy, organic jeans come in a variety of styles for men and women. Certified organic denim undergoes strict uniform standards that are verified by independent state or private organizations.

Raw Denim
This is pure cotton that has not been treated, distressed, washed, or broken down in any manner, other than dyeing it a color.

Raw denim usually has a very hard, stiff look and feel until it is completely broken in. It has very little or no stretch; it normally molds to the body after wearing several times. The best examples of raw denim are the oldies from 1940s and 1950s. These babies could survive any natural disaster and still maintain their beauty.

Blended Denim
Often, denim is combined with other fibers to manipulate the durability of the denim.

Stretch denim is a mixture of cotton denim and a stretch fabric, for example, Lycra or spandex. It helps create superb form-fitting and body-hugging jeans. Polyester is added to prevent shrinkage. Ramie-blended jeans are known for their ability to hold shape and their reduced wrinkling, and ramie introduces a silky luster. The types of denim blends are endless. And it's not unusual to find a blend of several different fibers, such as a ramie/cotton/poly/spandex blend.

Premium Denim
Generally used on designer jeans, premium denim provides a superior fit and styling.

The denim is higher quality, often coming from Japan and Italy. The different washes can add to the cost of a pair of jeans. Premium denims are not just limited to a great fit and different washes. They are detailed with different cuts and ornate with very intricate appliqués, topstitching, and diverse curving seams and layering.

Caring for Your Denim

Denim requires some attention when laundering. It bleeds, it fades, it shrinks and stretches, and it frays naturally. To prevent it bleeding onto other garments, wash it separately until you notice the wash water remains clear. To preserve the color and maintain the finish, wash inside out and add a cup of white vinegar to the rinse.

Embellished denim is best cared for by hand washing or dry cleaning to avoid color loss or damage to ornaments. You also might want to wash a new pair of jeans before wearing them to eliminate any sizing in the fabric, which can create unwanted stiffness.

Breaking Down Your Denim

Great denim finishes and washes are cool but often costly. You can break down your denim in the comfort of your own home. All you need is fabric softener, your denim, detergent, a clean sneaker, and a little patience. By this inexpensive and effective method, your jeans will feel softer and look older. A terrific characteristic of denim is its ability to naturally distress itself. Washing breaks down the fibers, creating a softer, more comfortable feel and fit.

Easy as pie, follow these steps:

1. Fill your washing machine with hot water and add the fabric softener of your choice.
2. Place garment into machine, let soak for 12 hours or more, add detergent, and run through wash cycle.
3. Machine dry and, for additional distressing, run the garment through dryer cycle along with a clean sneaker.
4. Repeat until the hand of the denim feels great to you.

Keeping Those Special Jeans Forever

If there is history behind your jeans, a special moment of your life when you wore them that makes it impossible for you and your jeans to part, you may hesitate to cut them up. Please don't fret. Look at your old denim as a catalyst for preserving the old while creating the new. You will be making something individual and more current, while preserving a piece of your past.

Best Jeans for the Bottom Half

When we hit the jackpot, the perfect pair of jeans will lift our buttocks (superb), elongate our legs (nice), firm our thighs (perfecto), and shape our hips in perfect proportion to the rest of our body. They get nonstop usage in our wardrobe. Here's a quick rundown on the styles that transform your body type into a work of art.

The Hourglass
A curvy body type with balanced hip and shoulder width and a defined waist.

We want to applaud your curves with hip-skimming styles. Try low-waist, flat-front jeans that ease into a full straight-leg trouser or boot cut. Avoid skinny and cigarette legs—they'll make you look wide hipped and heavy bottomed.

The Triangle
A pear-shaped body type with shoulders narrower than the hips, a slim torso and ribcage, a small waist, and full lower hips.

Wear boot-cut jeans, wide-leg and trouser jeans, wide-leg culottes, and cargo jeans. The slightly flared bottom minimizes thighs and behind, and balances out a wide hip or rear. Creating the balance is what we love. Wear low-waist, flat-front jeans with minimal details. Try a straight but full leg that gives you a relaxed fit through the hip and thigh. Lose the extravagant front and back pockets, as they bring unwanted attention to the hips.

The Inverted Triangle
A boyish athletic frame, with average-to-broad shoulders wider than your hips, and a straight, narrow waist.

Choose from a gamut of styles. Your boyish figure welcomes the variety: boot-cut, skinny, wide, relaxed, capri, and straight legs. Unlike most body types, inverted triangles can wear cigarette or skinny jeans. The slender cut at the calves makes hips look wider and adds curves to a flat behind. Counterbalance skinny jeans with a voluminous top, and always accompany them with a higher-heeled shoe such as a knee-high boot, classic pump, or strapped sandal.

The Rectangle
Straight up and down with hips and shoulders balanced and no defined waistline.

Wear denim with wide, flared, boot-cut, or straight legs. Avoid jeans that flatten your bottom. Stay away from jeans that are either too tight or too loose.

The Circle
Full figured and voluptuous, hips and shoulders are balanced with no defined waistline.

Wear jeans at your natural waist. It lengthens your legs as well as your torso. Hip-skimming styles with full legs and relaxed styles through the leg (wide leg, classic cuts, trouser denim, boot cut, or subtly flared legs) complement you. These styles create balance and the illusion of a defined waist. Avoid pleats or anything with tapered ankles, and hip huggers, low risers, cigarette or skinny legs, and high-waisted jeans.

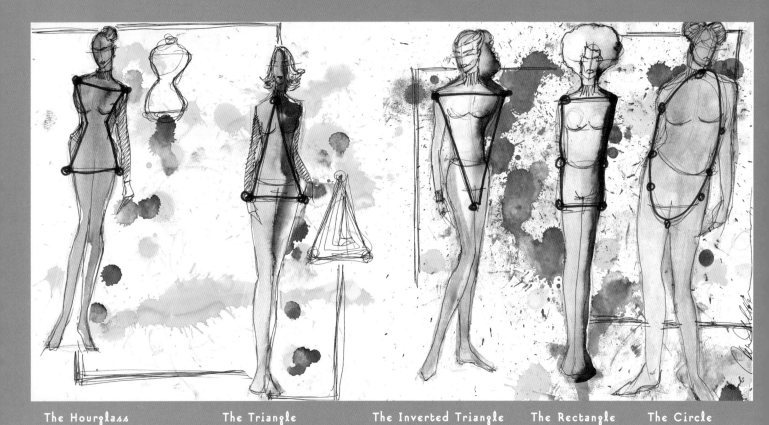

The Hourglass   The Triangle   The Inverted Triangle   The Rectangle   The Circle

Quick Cheats

For Long Legs: To lengthen legs, wear higher-waist trouser jeans to provide a longer vertical line. High-heeled shoes also make your legs look longer.

Say Yes! If you have narrower hips and slim legs, you can wear every style—wide, straight, cargo, skinny, cigarette, and boot cut.

Say No! If your butt is flat, watch out for low risers, which will appear to make your bottom look even flatter.

Understanding the styles and cuts before revamping your denim is essential. We have chosen authentic vintage denim jeans for the projects in this book. Therefore, the waists are a little higher than their low-riding counterparts. Not to worry, all the styles look fierce on a natural waist as well as the low hip.

Adorn Your Denim

Release your inner fashion designer, pour your heart into your denim canvas, and self-express, even if you are not ready to destroy and remake your denims. Here are things you can do without cutting the fabric and if you don't want glamorous, strategically placed hot-girl rips in your jeans. Adorning your denim is just as serious as the jean itself. Embellishing your denim can be as exciting as purchasing vintage jeans or finding an old pair in your closet! Here are techniques you can use when decorating your denim. Dare to add your flair.

A Basic: Transferring Designs to Denim

First, draw your pattern, shape, or image on paper.

Then, place dressmaker's tracing paper between the denim and the original drawing, with the ink side of the tracing paper facing the denim. Roll over the lines of the original drawing, using the tracing wheel. You can also sketch directly on the denim, using tailor's chalk (it's good for sketching because it's easy to erase mistakes). Freely mix and match any of these techniques. You can then adorn the denim, following the tracings, using paint, stitching, glue, beads, studs, fabrics, appliqués, trims, etc. Lay low or exaggerate your adornment. Blank denim gives voice to our innate desire to share and be heard.

APPLIQUÉ

Appliqués can totally transform the look of your denim to give it extra flair. You can purchase them or create your own using scraps of fabric, lace, or leather. Even artificial flowers can be easily adhered to denim for a fun, feminine look. Literally thousands of packaged appliqués are available and if you have certain themes in mind, your local fabric shop or craft store will probably have exactly what you need. (You can also buy them on the Internet). Appliqués are easy to sew on by hand, and are an extremely inexpensive way to funk up a garment.

BEDAZZLE

Make your denim ornate by using gems, crystals, beads, rhinestones, and other glitzy stones. Denim encrusted with jewels is almost standard for fabulousness. If you're a die-hard gem lover, purchase a Bedazzler (www.mybedazzler.com). This tool secures the jewel to the denim easily and quickly. You can also use a glue gun or fabric jewel glue to adhere the jewels to your denim apparel. Create a pattern or freestyle it. As you go with the flow, open your mind and transfer your bedazzling inspiration onto your denim clothes!

BUTTONS

Buttons are an inexpensive and easy way to decorate denim. Just about anybody can learn to sew on a button. There are so many varieties of buttons available today. Fabric and notions stores carry full ranges, from plain and simple plastic buttons to stone-encrusted metal ones to those made from wood, horn, or shells, and they come in a myriad of sizes and shapes. Antique buttons are always a good find, and a lot of them are one-of-a-kind. (Flea markets and garage sales are great places to find old buttons.)

DISTRESSING

You'll need only a pair of scissors, a sand block, and an awl (pointed tool for making holes) to distress virgin denim. This process is irreversible, so you'll want to start slowly and carefully, building to the desired stress level in small steps—distress a little, stop and look at it, distress a little more, look at it again, and so forth. Use the sand block to abrade the denim, breaking down the woven fibers so they are thinner and more pliable. Use scissors and an awl to rip, slash, and tear the denim, but be sure to first mark those rips, slashes, and tears onto the denim fabric, then cut, rip, and slash to perfection.

HARDWARE

Glamour punk has a place on the fashion chart. Use hardware to wild out your denim and take it from sweet to dangerous. Adding safety pins, grommets, eyelets, and studs is classic rock and roll. Try all shapes and sizes. You can buy kits, complete with the hardware and the tool(s) to attach it, at your local fabric or craft store. (Be sure to mark your design onto the denim before you start.)

LEATHER

Leather can make your denim rock. For luxurious leather embellishment, cut out the shape you desire and glue it onto the denim with fabric glue. When the glue dries, whipstitch the edges (or use some other decorative stitch). Make sure to use a new, sharp needle. (There are handsewing needles especially designed for denim and leather.) Note: Once leather is added, the garment becomes dry clean only.

PATCHWORK

Patchwork consists of varied colored patches of material sewn together, as in a quilt. Fabric patches on denim (and on jeans particularly) is very retro—it's a staple of the '70s that we love—elaborate, funky, and quirky. Use scraps of various fabrics to create a mural on your denim. Put a little bit of fabric glue on the fabric piece to secure it to the denim, then stitch around the outside edge of the patch onto the denim.

TRIMS

Trims are another way to decorate and embellish denim. Trims, especially flat, braided, and woven trims, are often added to the hems of denim clothing, but trims are not limited to edges. Lace, ribbons, tassels, cording, and feathers are all trims that can be used to jazz up your plain denim, anywhere on the garment. Use ribbon as a drawstring on a pair of cargo jeans. Try adding a lace edging down the front of a jacket or along the seams. Experiment with tassels as charms hanging from the zipper of your denim jacket. Use cords to wrap or drape the legs of cigarette-leg jeans.

TOPSTITCHING

Topstitching is a decorative stitch often used to accent a certain detail on a garment, such as the edges of pockets and seams, or around appliqués, trims, patches, and other decorative elements. You can topstitch by hand, using embroidery thread and a heavy-duty needle (see pickstitching below), or on a sewing machine, using long, straight stitches, zigzags, and other decorative machine stitches. Use a contrasting thread color when adding a topstitched detail—if your denim is pale blue, use red, green, or copper thread. A small, topstitched detail can make a big impact.

PICKSTITCHING

A pickstitch is done by hand and is used as a decorative finishing detail, like the top-stitch. The pickstitch should never go through two layers of fabric, just through the single layer you are adorning; when used to ornament thick fabrics like denim, some-times the pickstitches don't even go through to the back side of the single layer. Pickstitches should be short (⅛ to ¼ inch) with ¼ to ½ inch between them. Embroidery floss is the best choice for pickstitching but heavy-duty 2-ply cotton threads can be used also.

PICKSTITCHING VS. TOPSTITCHING

The difference between pickstitching and topstitching is that pickstitching is always done by hand, whereas topstitching is normally done on the sewing machine. Top-stitching can also be made through two or more layers of fabric, but pickstitching never goes through more than one layer.

Mix It Up—Don't Be Matchy-Matchy!

When embellishing denim, don't be afraid to be a little edgy, or quirky, or even tacky at times. Many of us have a tendency to want to match everything, but with denim projects we can dare to be individual. Mixing colors and textures are amazingly easy ways to give pizzazz to any garment or outfit. Mix different fabric textures and/or prints together, combine the unexpected, such as lace with wool, leather with camouflage, jersey cotton knit (sweatshirt material) with denim scraps, silk with cashmere, piqué cotton with corduroy...the list is endless. I will never forget something my art teacher told us in elementary school: "Do not be afraid to be tacky. It works, actually."

P atience is the single most important ingredient in achieving the result you want from your denim projects. Please take the time to read through the instructions for each project from start to finish before you actually begin working.

In addition to patience, there are other fundamental techniques and tools that you'll use over and over in every project in this book, and they are all spelled out here in detail. You'll find this section to be a great reference as you are working on the individual projects.

Supplies and Equipment

H aving the proper equipment and supplies on hand when creating your projects will make the world of difference. Here are all the basics you'll need.

Essential Supplies and Equipment (Needed for Every Project)

Aleene's Fabric Glue

Embroidery scissors or thread clippers

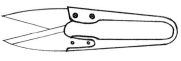

Scissors
(we recommend you invest in a good, high-quality pair)

Handsewing needles
(various sizes)
Heavy-duty straight pins
(ball heads optional)
Iron and ironing board
Marking devices
tailor's chalk, or fabric marking pen or pencil, or dress-maker's tracing paper and tracing wheel
Measuring devices
cloth tape measure, plastic drafting ruler (clear), curved ruler or French curve

Seam ripper

Sewing machine and sewing machine needles (14 and 16 pt for medium-weight fabrics, 18 pt for heavy-weight denim)
Thread, cotton-covered polyester or mercerized cotton (such as Coats & Clark Dual Duty Plus All-Purpose thread for medium-weight fabrics or Dual Duty Plus Topstitching thread for denim.)

Bias tape (off-white or black)
"D-fuzz-it" (knit razor)

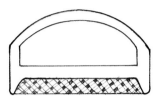

Ironing ham or roll
Iron on hemming tape

Pinking shears

French curve

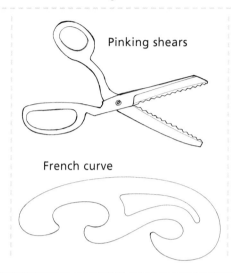

Safety glasses or goggles to
protect your eyes while
sewing (when sewing over
thick surfaces, needles can
occasionally snap off and
fly outward; it is important
to protect your eyes)
Sewing weights
(really heavy books
do the job just as well)
Tracing paper
Patternmaking paper

Measuring Basics

Taking proper measurements is crucial for the perfect fit. We suggest having a friend take your body part measurements, as it's easier for someone else to be accurate than when you take your own. It is critical to get these measurements right, in order to get the perfect fit in your reconstructed denim fashions.

Here are the body part measurements you need to take before you begin your projects. You won't need every one of these measurements for every project; each project uses some and not others. When measuring body parts, use only a cloth or plastic dressmaker's tape measure, not a retractable metal measuring tape. And have pen or pencil and paper handy to write down those measurements. Here are the body parts you'll need to measure for various projects:

The Right
Tape Measure
Always use a dressmaker's tape measure when measuring body parts. Dressmaker's tape measures are made from cloth or plastic and are designed to lie flat as they wrap around curves and under and over body parts. They come in a variety of colors, and are available at sewing and craft stores and on the Internet.

For Shirts, Tops,
and Jackets
Bust
High Bust
Waist
Hip (only needed
    for hip-length
    and longer tops)
Center Front
    Length

Center Back
    Length
Shoulder Width
Shoulder Length
Side Length

For Sleeves
Arm Length
Wrist Circum-
    ference

Armhole and
    Sleeve Cap

For Skirts
Waist
Natural Hip
Lower Hip
Skirt Length

For Pants
Waist
Natural Hip
Lower Hip
Pant's Length
Thigh

How to Take Body Measurements

Measuring your body parts (e.g., bust, waist, hips, etc.) is the main component in determining the final body measurements you'll use in the projects that follow, but there are two additional components you need to account for in your final body measurements—seam allowance and ease.* We use ½-inch seam allowances in our projects (unless otherwise specified). Wearing ease is generally 2 inches total (1 inch each for front and for back).

Here's an easy-to-remember formula:

Body Part Measurement + Seam Allowance + Ease = Your Body Measurement.

FRONTS AND BACKS

In any overall body part measurement, the halves are rarely equal. For example, while an overall waist might measure 30 inches, the front waist could be 16½ inches and the back waist 13½; a total bustline might measure 39 inches, with the front being 19 inches and the back 17. Therefore, you will measure the front and the back of your body separately for most of the following.

Please note that you will not need every one of these measurements in any single project.

It is critical that you keep your tape measure straight and level when measuring body parts.

TAKING MEASUREMENTS FOR SHIRTS, TOPS, JACKETS, SLEEVES, SKIRTS, AND PANTS

It is best to take your measurements wearing only undergarments, or fitted leggings and a tank top. Before you begin, you'll need to mark side seam lines (on whatever you are wearing for the measurements—bra, panties, leggings, skin, etc.), using an erasable/washable pencil or marker. This side seam mark should be the halfway point between the front and back of the body, on the sides of the torso, waist, hips, and thighs (i.e., where the side seams of the shirts, pants, and skirts will fall). This way, you will be measuring from the same side seam point when you measure the front and the back of each body part.

Please note that the ease measurements given below are for fitted garments. For looser fitting garments, add more ease.

The basic body measurements (numbers 1–20) are "constants" that don't change from project to project (things like waist, hip, bust, etc.) The other measurements (armholes, sleeve cap, length, etc.) will change from project to project. You'll use these measurements to make adjustments in the garments you are reworking to make them fit you the way you want.

You could not wear a garment that measured exactly the same as your body part measurements. A little extra room is required to allow you to walk, sit, and otherwise move in your clothes. This extra room is known as ease, or wearing ease.

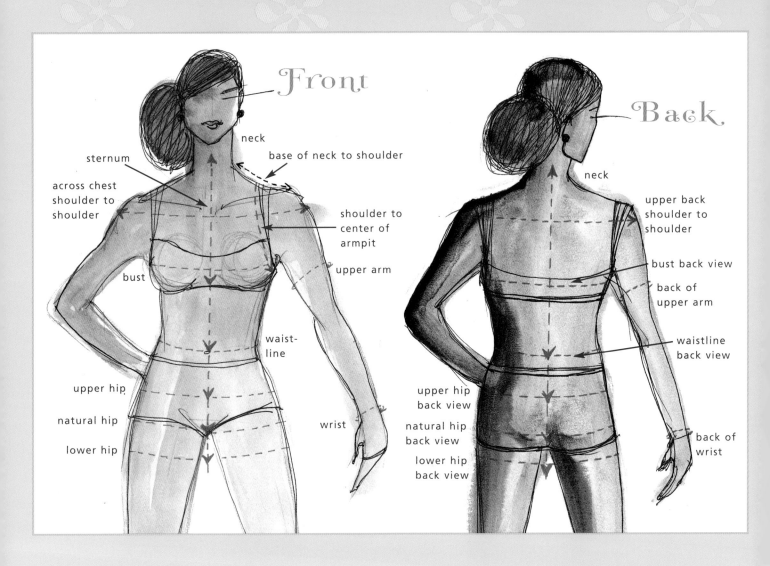

Front

neck
base of neck to shoulder
sternum
across chest
shoulder to
shoulder
shoulder to
center of
armpit
upper arm
bust
waist-
line
upper hip
natural hip
wrist
lower hip

Back

neck
upper back
shoulder to
shoulder
bust back view
back of
upper arm
waistline
back view
upper hip
back view
natural hip
back view
lower hip
back view
back of
wrist

Be sure to write all your body measurements down as you take them, *and don't forget to add the appropriate seam allowance and ease to each measurement*, as indicated. There is even space to record each of your body measurements, right in this book.

1. **MEASURING NECK:** Measure around the base of your neck, where the neck meets the shoulders. Measure front and back neck separately. Add a 1-inch seam allowance and ½-inch ease to the front neck and also to the back neck.
Front Neck _____ Back Neck _____

2. **MEASURING FRONT BUST:** (You must wear a bra when measuring front bust, unless you never wear a bra.) On front of body, measure across fullest part of bust from side seam to side seam. Add 1-inch seam allowance and 1-inch ease.
_____

3. **MEASURING BACK BUST:** Measure across back of body from side seam to side seam at exact same level you did for the front bust. Add 1-inch seam allowance and 1-inch ease. _____

4. **MEASURING FRONT HIGH BUST:** Measure straight across front, about 3 inches down from the base of the neck (or about 3 inches up from the bust), from armhole to armhole. Add 1-inch seam allowance and 1-inch ease. _____

5. **MEASURING BACK HIGH BUST:** Measure straight across back, at the exact same level as front high bust, from armhole to opposite armhole. Add 1-inch seam allowance and 1-inch ease. _____

6. **MEASURING BUSTLINE:** Measure down the center of the front of your body from the base of the neck to the level of the fullest part of the bust—the bustline (i.e., the nipple line.) _____

7. **MEASURING BUST POINT DISTANCE:** Measure from nipple to nipple, straight across the bustline. Add ½-inch ease. _____

8. **MEASURING FRONT WAIST:** At your natural waist (about navel level), measure across front of body, from side seam to side seam. Add 1-inch seam allowance and 1-inch ease. _____

9. **MEASURING BACK WAIST:** Measure across back waist, from side seam to side seam, at exact same level as front waist. Add 1-inch seam allowance and 1-inch ease. _____

10. **MEASURING FRONT NATURAL HIP AND FRONT LOWER HIP:** Front natural hip—At the side seam, measure 8–9 inches down from your natural waist to determine natural hip level. At this point, measure across front hipline from side seam to side seam. Add 1-inch seam allowance and 1-inch ease.

FRONT LOWER HIP—At the side seam, measure 11 inches down from your natural waist. At this point, measure across front lower hip from side seam to side seam. Add 1-inch seam allowance and 1-inch ease. _____

11. **MEASURING BACK NATURAL HIP AND THE BACK LOWER HIP:** Back natural hip—Measure across back hip from side seam to side seam at exact same level as front natural hip. Add 1-inch seam allowance and 1-inch ease. _____
BACK LOWER HIP—Measure across back hip from side seam to side seam at exact same level as front lower hip (i.e., 11 inches below natural waist). Add 1-inch seam allowance and 1-inch ease. _____

12. **MEASURING CENTER FRONT LENGTH:** Measure from the base of the neck, down the center front, to the natural waistline. _____

13. **MEASURING CENTER BACK LENGTH:** Measure from the nape of the neck, down the center back (i.e., spine), to the natural waistline. _____

14. **MEASURING FRONT SHOULDER WIDTH:** Measure from the edge of the shoulder across the front upper chest to same position at opposite side. Add 1 inch for ease. _____

15. **MEASURING BACK SHOULDER WIDTH:** Measure from the edge of the shoulder across the back to the same position on the opposite side. Add 1 inch for ease. _____

16. **MEASURING BACK SHOULDER BLADES:** Measure across the back, about 4 inches down from the nape of the neck, from back armhole edge to the same point on the other side. Add 1 inch for ease. _____

17. **MEASURING SHOULDER LENGTH:** Measure the length of the shoulder from the neck to the end of the shoulder. _____

18. **MEASURING SIDE LENGTH:** On the side of torso, measure from about 2 inches below the armpit down the side to the waistline. _____

19. **MEASURING ARM LENGTH:** With arm relaxed and hanging down from shoulder, measure along side of arm from top of shoulder, down to elbow, and then from elbow down to wrist bone. (Note that as your arm hangs down in a relaxed way, it will bend a bit at the elbow. Do not lock your elbow when taking this measurement; keep it relaxed and bent.) Add 1-inch seam allowance and 1-inch ease. _____

20. **MEASURING WRIST CIRCUMFERENCE:** Wrap tape measure around wrist bone, then add 1-inch seam allowance and ease as desired. _____

21. **MEASURING ARMHOLE CIRCUMFERENCE:** This is a measurement you do not take on your body. The best way to accurately measure armhole circumference is to measure the armholes of the actual shirt you are working on. Measure the front armhole and the back armhole separately: Lay the shirt flat on a tabletop, front side up, smoothing all wrinkles. Measure from the underarm seam, up around curve of armhole to the shoulder seam at top of armhole. Add 1-inch seam allowance. Repeat for back of armhole. _____

22. **MEASURING SLEEVE CAPS:** The sleeve cap is determined by the armhole circumference, plus ease. Sleeve cap ease is distributed across the entire top of the sleeve cap (there is no ease in the underarm portion of the sleeve). The amount of ease will vary depending on the style of the sleeve. A puffed sleeve requires a lot of extra ease (at least 4 inches), whereas an average, more fitted sleeve cap would only need 1 inch of ease. Be sure to add 1-inch seam allowance to the sleeve cap measurement. _____

23. **MEASURING SKIRT LENGTH:** Hold tape measure on side seam at natural waistline, and let the tape measure hang free, dropping to floor. Note desired length (above, at, or below knee level.) Add something for the hem (2 inches for a traditional turned hem) and $\frac{1}{2}$-inch seam allowance at waist. Remember to wear whatever shoes you will wear with the garment when taking skirt length measurements. _____

24. **MEASURING PANT LENGTH:** Hold tape measure on side seam at natural waistline, and let the tape measure hang free, dropping to floor. Note the desired length: above, below, or at knee; capri length; ankle length; or floor length. Add $\frac{1}{2}$-inch seam allowance at waist, and hem measurement at bottom (2 inches for a traditional turned hem). Remember to wear whatever shoes you will wear with the garment when taking pant length measurements. _____

25. **MEASURING THIGHS:** Measure completely around upper thigh at its widest point, being sure to keep tape measure flat and level. Add 1-inch seam allowance and ease as desired (1 inch for fitted thigh, more inches for looser fit). _____

If you are taking your own measurements,* you MUST stand in front of a full-length mirror to measure yourself. Use the mirror as your tool to help you place the tape measure in the correct position on each body part and to make sure the tape measure is straight and level as it wraps around your body.

If someone else is taking your measurements, stand directly in front of the person who is taking your measurements, at the same level.

Allow your arms to hang naturally. Do not raise your arms in the air or pull them away from your sides. Allow for a small space under your arms to slide the tape measure around bust. Even when taking the bust measurement, your arms should hang naturally by your sides.

Stand in a relaxed position while maintaining an upright posture; do not slouch or bend or twist your body while taking measurements.

Do not pull the tape measure too tight or too loose. It should lie flat against the body, and be completely level as it runs across your body. If it dips, it's too loose; if it rises up, it's too tight.

Do not hold your breath or suck in your stomach when measuring your waist. When measuring for skirt or pant length, allow the tape measure to hang freely to your desired length. Do not pull it taut to that length.

When measuring for skirt or pant lengths, consider the heel height of the shoe or boot you'll wear with the garment. Wear that shoe or boot when taking these measurements. You can also measure the lengths of your own skirts and pants.

Measuring a Fitted Shirt

As an alternative to measuring your body parts, you can take measurements for shirts, tops, and jackets from your favorite fitted shirt, as long as the shirt really does fit you perfectly. (Note: Do not use a knit shirt, only a woven shirt, as denim does not stretch.) Be sure to press the shirt and lay it flat, smoothing out all wrinkles and making sure seam lines are straight. Make sure you add 1-inch seam allowances and something for ease to the measurements.

Marking

You'll need just a few basic tools to mark the cutting and sewing lines for your projects. All these materials are available in sewing and craft shops and on the Internet.

Marking Tools
FABRIC MARKING PENS, PENCILS, OR TAILOR'S CHALK

The new air-soluble and wash-away pens and pencils for marking fabrics are great to use because their pointed tips make accurate marks, and the marks themselves are easy to erase because they are temporary, not permanent. Air-soluble markers disappear over time. Water-soluble inks (wash-away inks) can be washed away with water. Test all markers before using them, because some inks are permanently set by heat.

Taking your own measurements is challenging because some areas of the body are so hard to reach. For the most accurate measurements, it is best to have another person do it for you.

Be sure to read the packaging of your purchased markers carefully to make sure they are temporary.

When selecting marking pencils, use white, yellow, or light blue, as these colors wash out and erase more easily than darker pencil colors. (You can use a regular #2 pencil for marking, but test it on your fabric first to make sure it erases or washes away easily.)

Use only white, yellow, or light blue tailor's chalk. We do not recommend red or black chalk as those colors do not iron out, wash out, or wipe off easily, as the lighter colors do. Use with a light touch and erase mistakes before re-marking (otherwise you won't remember which mark is right and which is the mistake).

DRESSMAKER'S TRACING PAPER AND TRACING WHEEL	Stick to the white, yellow, and light blue colors of dressmaker's tracing paper. Red and black tracing papers do not iron out, wash out, or wipe off easily, as the lighter colors do. (Do not use the black or dark blue carbon sheets you would use in office work, as they don't wash out and may permanently stain fabrics.) Always place the dressmaker's tracing paper with the marking side facing the fabric. You can place markings on both the right and left sides of fronts and backs simultaneously by placing a second sheet of tracing paper face up under the bottom layer. It often helps to have a plastic mat or piece of board underneath to keep the fabric from slipping as you roll the tracing wheel.
CLEAR RULERS	Clear rulers are the best because you can see seam lines, marking lines, and design details through them. You'll need just two rulers: a clear, curved or French curve ruler a plastic drafting ruler (18 x 2 inches)
TRACING PAPER AND PENCIL	Not needed for all projects, but handy for tracing designs and shapes you'll transfer to some projects.
How to Use Body Measurements to Mark Cutting Lines	Now that you've calculated the body measurements, here's how you transfer those measurements to the clothing and fabrics, and mark the cutting lines for the projects you make. Please refer to both the written instructions and the corresponding illustrations. Note that stitching lines (seam lines) will usually be ½ inch inside the cutting lines you mark, and therefore often don't have to be marked. The center front and center backs are the fold lines, and no seam allowances are added there.

• There are a few preparatory steps you need to take before you begin marking:

1. Read through the instructions for your project before you start marking, to pick up any special measurements or seam allowances. (Most of the time, seam allowances are ½ inch but occasionally we call for a smaller or larger seam allowance. Ease can vary depending on how tight or loose a particular garment fits.)

2. Make sure all your final body measurements include appropriate seam allowances and ease.

3. With an iron, press all garments and fabric pieces.

4. Work on a level, hard tabletop surface. (Working on the floor is too hard on your back and knees.)

5. Separate the fronts of shirts, tops, jackets, skirts, and pants from the backs along side seams either by cutting the side seams or by using a seam ripper. (For most T-shirt projects, you don't need to separate the fronts from the backs, because you'll cut them out simultaneously.)

6. Lay out pressed garment and fabric pieces flat, smoothing all wrinkles. Before marking, fold each front piece and back piece in half lengthwise (this will delineate the center front and center back of each garment.) You will mark and cut the front and back pieces separately. (Remember, the body part measurements may be different from front to back.)

7. Mark the cutting lines on the garment pieces while they are folded in half lengthwise.

8. Cut pieces while they are folded in half lengthwise. Most of the time, you will cut along cutting lines while the piece is folded in half lengthwise, i.e, through both layers of fabric, cutting the left and right sides of the piece simultaneously. (The instructions will tell you any time you should cut through a single layer only.)

9. Always, always use fabric scissors, not paper scissors, for cutting fabric. **Never, ever** use your fabric scissors to cut anything other than cloth, thread, elastic, and woven trims. Paper will dull the blades of your scissors, making fabric cutting a chore.

Start Marking

Now that you have recorded your body measurements, have read through the instructions for your project, and have prepped your garment pieces, you are ready to mark cutting lines on those pieces. Please follow both the text and the illustrations. The directions say to mark with tailor's chalk, but you may also mark with dressmaker's tracing paper and a tracing wheel, or fabric pen or pencil. Please use only those fabric markers and pens that disappear easily using an iron, eraser, or water. You can mark just the top layer of the fabric or the top and the bottom layers (by using a second sheet of dressmaker's tracing paper underneath).

The following instructions cover all the marking possibilities you'll encounter in the book. Please note that you'll only need to mark some of the following for any particular project. You may need to mark more or less depending on the fit of the garment you're reworking. (If the shoulders, sleeve caps, and armholes have the fit you want, you won't have to adjust them; if the waist and bust fit, you won't need to add any darts, etc.)

A word about darts: Because the bust and hips are almost always larger than the waist, you need to get rid of the excess fabric in the waist without completely eliminating the extra fabric needed for the bust or the hips; a dart does just that. Darts can be placed on the waistline, at the side seam, at the armhole, or at the shoulder. We'll show you how to mark them and how to sew them.

Since everything is cut on the fold, bust, waist, and both hip measurements should be divided by 4 to get the proper distance from center front and back folds. The shoulder to the center armpit is the only measurement that will remain the same. Now you will need to divide some of the measurements by 4 and others by 2. Why? Because when cutting you are to cut your projects using a center fold method.

Refer to complete measuring chart on page 20.

Refer to complete measuring chart on page 20.

Measurements to be divided by 4 are:		Measurements to be divided by 2 are:	
Bust	34" divided by 4 = 8½"	Across shoulder	17" divided by 2 = 8½"
Waist	27" divided by 4 = 6¾"	to shoulder front	
Upper Hip	35" divided by 4 = 8¾"		
Natural Hip	37" divided by 4 = 9¼"	Upper back	18" divided by 2 = 9"
Lower Hip	39" divided by 4 = 9¾"	shoulder to shoulder	

Once you have completed the math of your body measurement breakdown, mark your garment using the steps (below) in the illustrations (p. 27 top):

REMEMBER TO ALWAYS CUT GARMENTS WHILE FOLDED SO THAT YOU HAVE REFERENCE FROM CENTER FRONT OR BACK FOLD.

1. Once your garment is folded and pressed completely flat, using your bustline center front measurement (step 6, page 21) from base of neck to center or breast, make a very faint mark with tailor's chalk.

2. Then, from your first faint center front mark, measure out to the side of your bust measurement, and also make a faint mark at that point with tailor's chalk.

3. Follow the same procedure from step 2 to mark your side waist point on the folded garment.

4. Continue the same technique from steps 2 and 3 to mark your upper hip.

5. You now have three faint marks at the side of your folded front garment. Using tailor's chalk, connect the marks, which will create your side seam.

6. For your hemline, you may draw (A) a slight curve, or (B) a straight line.

REMEMBER: **All the measurements you use below must include the appropriate seam allowance and ease, which you added when you recorded your body measurements (see pages 20–22). Make sure the body measurements you are working with include the appropriate seam allowances and ease.**

REMEMBER: **You are working with the garment folded in half lengthwise, along the center front and/or the center back.**

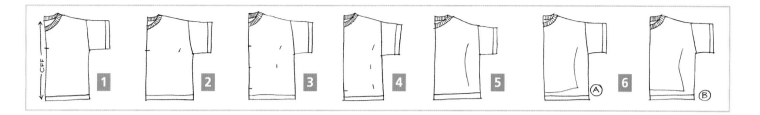

HOW TO USE
MEASUREMENTS
TO MARK ARMHOLE
CUTTING LINES

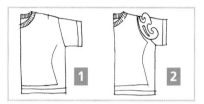

You must have previously marked your bust, waist, and upper hip, as well as have drawn your side seam before completing this step. Apply your previous body measurement as follows:

1. Using tailor's chalk, make a faint mark at your shoulder measurement.
2. Place a French curve ruler between the top shoulder mark and your side seam bust mark. Use the measurement markings on the ruler for your correct distance measurement from shoulder to armpit. Then with the tailor's chalk, trace along the ruler's edge for your armhole cutting line.

HOW TO USE
MEASUREMENTS
TO MARK BUST
DARTS

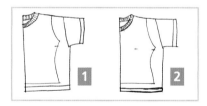

You must have already completed side seam and sleeve inset markings, as above, before completing the following steps.

1. Measure 1 inch down from the armhole on the side seam and make a faint mark, using tailor's chalk.
2. Then, make a faint mark using the tailor's chalk to center of bust. This measurement is your previously divided bust inches. For example, if it is 9″ then divide that by 2 = 4½″. Therefore you are marking in toward center of breast at 4½″.

For detailed illustration refer to step 4 of the Puffed-Sleeved Shirt.

Sleeves

You may be adjusting an existing sleeve, or creating one from scratch. In either case, you follow the same approach.

In order to mark cutting lines for sleeves, you have to know the armhole measurement, the sleeve length, the wrist circumference, and the type of sleeve cap (fitted or puffy). Basically, the measurement of the sleeve cap (i.e., the top of the sleeve) is equal to the total armhole length, plus ease (the more ease, the puffier the sleeve).

ADJUSTING AN EXISTING SLEEVE AND SLEEVE CAP: Unless the existing sleeve is very large, you probably won't be able to make a very puffy sleeve cap out of a fitted one (you'll have to do that from scratch). But you can adjust the length and shape of the sleeve cap to fit your new, adjusted armhole.

Fold sleeve in half lengthwise and, using chalk, mark lightly along folded edge; this is the center line of the sleeve. Open sleeve and lay it flat, with right side facing up. Note the front and the back of each sleeve. Using tape measure, measure around raw edges of front and back sleeve cap from underarms to shoulder seam. (The back sleeve cap, like the back armhole, will be longer than the front sleeve cap.) For fitted sleeve cap, add ¼-inch ease to front sleeve cap measurement and ½- to ¾-inch ease to back sleeve cap, and up to 2 inches to the front and 3 inches to the back for a puffy sleeve cap.

Take the front armhole measurement, including the ½-inch seam allowance and ¼-inch ease, and subtract it from the sleeve cap measurement taken above. If you are going for a fitted sleeve cap, the amount remaining needs to be trimmed from the sleeve cap. Let's say you need to lose 2 inches from the sleeve cap. At the center top of sleeve cap, mark down ½ inch to 1 inch. Using a curved ruler (with curve at top), mark a new, shorter sleeve cap from this lower point, blending the new sleeve cap line into the existing underarm curve. Measure sleeve cap. If the sleeve cap is still too long, lower the sleeve in ½-inch intervals until you get the measurement you want.

If you need to add inches to the sleeve cap, measure up from the center top of sleeve cap, mark, then draw new sleeve cap using a curved ruler, blending higher sleeve cap curve into existing underarm curve. (You'll have to use a little trial and error to get the exact measurement you want, but, if you raise a fitted sleeve cap by on a fitted cap by 1½ inch, you will get a gentle puffed sleeve.)

Sleeve cap ease is distributed across the top of the sleeve cap only, not across the underarm portion of the sleeve. Place a mark at each end of the sleeve cap, about 4 inches in from the underarm edge of the sleeve. You will distribute ease between the two points.

HOW TO DRAW A SLEEVE CAP   DRAWING A SLEEVE AND SLEEVE CAP FROM SCRATCH: As you can see, the sleeve cap looks a bit like a bell curve, (see page 42, Step 6) with gently sloping underarm curves at each end, and a high, rounded sleeve cap in the middle, between the underarm curves. The total sleeve cap length is equal to the length of the total armhole measurement, plus seam allowance and whatever ease is desired. The ease is distributed across the top of the sleeve cap when the sleeve is stitched in to the armhole, creating a sleeve cap that follows the curve of the arm and shoulder.

For some projects, you will create rather than adjust sleeves. The best way to draw a sleeve from measurements is to use an existing sleeve pattern (like one from a sewing pattern) or an old shirt sleeve as a foundation for your new sleeve pattern. Mark the sleeve centerline on the sleeve pattern or old sleeve, then lay it flat. Follow the instructions above for adjusting a sleeve cap and draw your new fitted (or puffy) cap directly on the pattern (or old sleeve). If you need to, tape extra paper or fabric to the top of the sleeve cap to accommodate a cap larger than the existing one.

Take this adjusted sleeve cap pattern and either transfer it to your fabric, using your choice of marking devices. (See detailed illustrations for drawing a puffed sleeve cap on pages 42 and 54.)

SLEEVE LENGTH: For a full-length sleeve, using the arm length, measure straight down from center of sleeve cap to wrist level (be sure to include hemming measurement); mark and draw sleeve bottom/hem line. Mark centerline at wrist level.

A number of our projects feature short sleeves. We find that a 4-inch length (from the *underarm* of sleeve cap, not the top of sleeve cap) works very well for our short-sleeved projects.

SLEEVE WIDTH: Determine how wide or narrow you want your sleeve to be. Add seam allowance, then divide by 2. At bottom hem of sleeve, on each side of center line, measure out that distance from the center line and mark. Connect these two end points with a straight or curved line, as you desire.

Skirt/Pants:

Instructions for using your body measurements to mark skirts and pants will be found in specific project instructions. If you are having trouble taking accurate body measurements, you can instead measure a pair of pants or a skirt that fit you perfectly. With all body measurements, be sure to add appropriate seam allowance and ease to measurements before marking cutting lines. In general, you'll want 2 inches total of ease around the bust, waist, and hips (that's 1 inch for the front and 1 inch for the back). For a looser fit, increase the ease. If you are working on the fronts and backs while they are folded in half lengthwise, remember to divide the front and back length measurements by 2.

Tips for Sewing Denim

Heavy-duty needles are a must! We suggest using denim needles, as the points are extra-sharp for easier penetration. If you're a type A denim revamper, begin every project with a new needle, as sewing on a tough fabric like denim dulls needles very fast. The heavier the denim, the larger the needle size required.

We recommend using a thimble and a larger "sharp" or embroidery needle when handsewing. When embellishing, sometimes we choose to handsew; other times, we use a sewing machine. When handsewing, you do not need to penetrate the entire fabric. Sew atop the fabric, since the ornaments are on the outermost layer.

Basting and Gathering

Basting is a temporary stitch used to hold two fabric pieces together until they can be stitched together permanently. It is also used to create gathers along a fabric edge. We recommend using brightly colored thread for this technique so that when you have finished basting or gathering it is easy to remove the thread.

HOW TO HAND BASTE: Using a handsewing needle and thread, take large running stitches (½ to 1 inch; ½ to 1 inch apart), about ¼ to ⅜ inch from raw edge, either through a single layer of fabric (for gathering), or two or more layers (for seams and other construction details).

HOW TO BASTE USING A SEWING MACHINE: Every machine has a stitch length control function. Some machines give you a stitch length number; others have an actual basting stitch setting. To baste a seam or other construction detail, use the longest machine stitch length available and machine baste fabric layers together inside the seam allowance (for example, with ½-inch seam allowance, machine baste ⅜ inches in from raw edges).

GATHERING: Gathering is a process of using long stitches to draw up a length of fabric into a shorter length, creating soft even folds and extra room. You'll often find gathering in sleeve caps, under the bust, at the bottoms of sleeves, anywhere you want to add fullness to a garment for either wearing ease or aesthetic appeal. You can gather along an entire seam line, or part of one. Gathering is very easy to do, either by hand or by using a sewing machine. Before you gather, mark the points at which the gathering should start and stop.

HAND GATHERING: Hand baste through a single layer of fabric about ¼ inch in from the raw edge. Pull threads from each end (like pulling a drawstring) until gathered piece is the desired length. Secure threads at ends by knotting them or wrapping around a pin. Adjust gathers, distributing them evenly between gathering points.

MACHINE GATHERING: Some machines have a preset gathering stitch that stitches and gathers the fabric simultaneously. Otherwise, using the longest stitch length on your sewing machine, stitch between gathering points ¼ inch in from raw edge. Pull the threads at each end (like a drawstring) until gathered piece is the desired length. Secure thread ends as above. Adjust gathers, distributing them evenly between gathering points. You have the option of doing basting stitch by machine. However we prefer to do it by hand using a bright contrasting color thread. This is much easier to remove, and it will not blend into the fabric. Basting stitches done by hand are much easier to remove. You also do not have to keep changing the settings on your machine. That can often get confusing and cause mistakes.

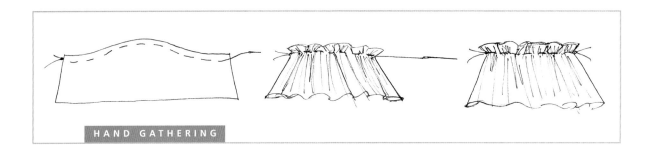

HAND GATHERING

Sewing Pleats and Tucks

Like gathering, tucks and pleats are another way to add volume and interest. They can also be used ornamentally, as styling details. Tucks and pleats are generally made to show on the outside of the garment. You'll find them on sleeves (at both caps and hems), at waistlines (high and low, on dresses, pants, and skirts), and at the center backs of jackets, shirts, and skirts (try walking in a pencil skirt that doesn't have a kick pleat). There are many ways to fold and sew tucks and pleats, so experiment to find the look you like best. Remember that tucks and pleats use extra fabric—even the simplest 1-inch pleat uses 2 inches of fabric, so account for that when placing them.

PLEATS: There are many types of pleats: side pleats, box pleats, inverted pleats, accordion pleats, and pleats with underlays. Though markings for the different types vary, all pleats require a fold line and a placement line. Each pleat is folded along its fold line, then brought over to line up with its corresponding placement line. The folded section between the fold and pleat lines is the underfold. In general, the amount of fabric needed for a pleat is double the pleat size. In other words, a 2-inch width pleat requires 4 inches of fabric, 2 inches for the pleat and 2 inches for the underlay. (Your pleat and underlay can be different measurements if you desire; just keep them consistent when marking.) To mark pleat fold and placement lines, determine the area where the pleats will go.

Divide that measurement by the pleat + underlay measurement, to determine the number of pleats that will fit. (Or, divide the pleat area measurement by the number of pleats desired to get the pleat/underlay size.) Always pleat on a single layer of fabric. Mark the fold and placement lines parallel to each other and parallel to the grainline,

on the right or wrong side of the fabric, as you desire. Fold each pleat along fold line and bring the folded edge over to the placement line and match the two lines; pin or baste; press. (You can fold the pleat either to the right or the left. With inverted pleats, you'll bring two fold lines into one center placement line.) Once all pleats have been folded, basted, and pressed, you can topstitch for a short distance (2–5 inches) along the pleat fold line, or not, if desired.

TUCKS: At tuck location, mark two parallel tuck stitching lines (parallel to each other and to the grain line of fabric). The width of the tuck is half the distance between the stitching lines. If tuck is to be on outside of garment, mark the right side of fabric; if tuck is to be on inside of garment, mark on wrong side of fabric. Fold tuck to inside or outside (as marked), matching stitching lines; stitch along stitching lines the length of the tuck. Lay fabric flat. Press tuck flat, to the right or left of stitching line, you can also topstitch close to pressed folded edge, if desired.

Finishes for Edges, Seams, and Hems

You can finish raw edges of seams, pockets, sleeves, hems, waistbands, in a variety of ways. In our projects, we like our edges, hems, and seams in their raw form, because the raw edges of denim fray evenly over time and we like that aesthetic.

FRAYED SEAMS OR EDGES: Frayed seams can be on the inside or, if you like the look, on the outside of the garment. Stitch seam to appear on either the right side or the wrong side of fabric, depending on whether you want your frayed seams to show; press open and flat. Allow them to fray over time. You can do a small to medium straight stitch, or a small zigzag stitch very, very close to the seam or stitching line to keep the frayed edge from encroaching on seam lines themselves. You can cut edges with a straight scissor or pinking shears. (Pinked edges will fray less and more slowly.) If you don't want your seam edges to fray, sew a straight stitch or a zigzag stitch about ¼ inch in from the raw edge.

PINKED SEAMS OR EDGES: The easiest seam finish is a pinked edge. Simply trim the seam allowance with pinking shears (or cut out the piece using pinking shears instead of scissors). The zigzagged edge helps to prevent raveling. Sew a straight stitch just below the pinking, to prevent further fraying. If sewing by hand, pink the edge and then handsew a zigzag stitch to prevent further raveling.

ZIGZAGGED SEAMS OR EDGES: You can also prevent further fraying by zigzag stitching ¼ inch from the raw edges of the seam, either through both layers or through one layer at a time. (Some people like to zigzag stitch around all raw edges before construction.)

SERGED SEAMS OR EDGES: A serger is a sewing machine that trims the seam allowance and then overcasts the raw edges of the seam with a V-shaped stitch as you sew. This is a good stitch for denim, as it makes the seam less bulky.

BINDING SEAMS OR EDGES: Bind the seam allowances with double-fold bias tape: After stitching the seam, cover the raw edges of the seam with double-fold bias tape; topstitch folded edge closest to seamline.

FINISHED HEMS: If you would prefer a finished hem on your projects, you are welcome to do so. Just remember to add the hem measurement to the finished length of your piece. A simple hem: Fold fabric edge over ⅜ inch toward wrong side, then fold again ½ inch. From wrong side, topstitch (by machine) close to folded edge, or, hand stitch using a blind stitch. (To blind stitch a hem: take a tiny stitch in the garment, then bring the needle up diagonally through the fold of the hem edge, all around the hem, keeping stitches about ¼ to ½ inch apart.)

TUNNEL HEMS: On some projects, we finish the hems of pants, skirts, blouses, and sleeves with a drawstring. This serves a double function as both the hem and a fashion statement. To make the "tunnel" for the cord, rope, or ribbon drawstring, add ½ inch to the width of the drawstring; this is your hem width. Fold the hem width to the wrong side of the garment, pin, and stitch with straight stitch ¼ inch from raw edge (leaving ¼ inch of ease inside the tunnel, so the drawstring can move smoothly). Be sure to leave an opening in the sewn hem so you can insert the drawstring and run it through the tunnel. (More details on tunnel hems are given in specific projects.)

- -

NO-SEW HEMS   FABRIC GLUE: Measure hem. Spread a thin layer of fabric glue on wrong side of hem, close to raw edge. Fold hem to wrong side along hemline, pressing raw edge with fingers so hem edge adheres to wrong side of fabric. Allow to dry before wearing. (You can also topstitch the hem once the glue has dried, if desired.)

IRON-ON HEMMING TAPE: Cut piece of iron-on hemming tape the same length as hem. Fold hem along hemline toward wrong side of garment. Sandwich hemming tape between wrong side of hem and wrong side of garment, ⅛ to ¼ inch from raw edge of hem. Fuse layers together using a hot, dry iron.

- -

How to Reinforce Seams with Twill Tape

Also known in the fashion industry as fabric tape, twill tape comes in different widths. We recommend using ¼-inch-wide tape for most of the projects in this book. Twill tape is generally used on more fragile fabrics as reinforcement so the needle of the sewing machine does not rip the fabric, and is perfect for old or extremely worn garments that are being reconstructed or deconstructed. Remember to use a dark-colored tape on colored fabrics and light-colored tape on white or cream fabrics.

1. Pin the two pieces to be joined together, centering the twill tape on the seam stitching line of the top piece.

2. Machine stitch seam together by stitching down the center of the twill tape through both pieces and tape at the same time.

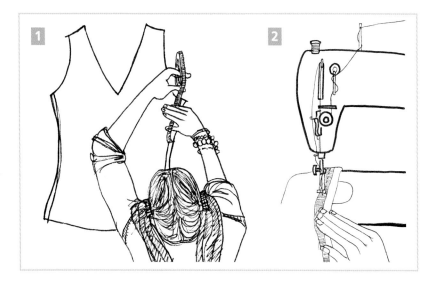

Gluing Basics

Fabric Glue

Fabric glue is a fantastic shortcut tool for denim projects. We have suggested throughout the projects to use glue, to save time as well as wear and tear on your sewing machines and even more on your hands.

You can use fabric glue instead of pins to secure seams before stitching, and to adhere pockets and other embellishments to the garment before stitching them on. You can also use fabric glue to secure hems without stitching them. We recommend you use Aleene's Fabric Glue (available in craft and sewing stores, and on the Internet) because it adheres well, doesn't dry stiff, and doesn't wash away with repeated laundering.

Here are some basic rules about using glue:

1. Work on a flat, even surface when gluing.
2. Your fabric surface should be clean and free of any debris.
3. Never use too much glue. It is best to spread a thin layer of glue on both surfaces to be bonded. Do it in the same manner as buttering toast. We suggest using some sort of spreading tool, such as a Popsicle stick, a wooden coffee stirrer, or a strip of cardboard about ½-inch wide and 4 or 5 inches long, cut from an old shoebox.
4. Allow the glue to get tacky. In other words, after applying a thin layer of glue to both surfaces, wait 30 seconds before placing the fabrics together. If you are in a room that has great circulation like a ceiling fan or a cross breeze because the windows are open, then only wait about 20 seconds before placing the fabrics together.
5. Once your two fabric surfaces are glued together, put something heavy on top of the piece: books, or sewing weights if you have them. Leave it like this for about 20 to 30 minutes, for secure glue bonding.
6. Always place a piece of cardboard or paper between layers when gluing something to just the top layer of fabric. Otherwise, the glue will seep through all layers and bond layers you don't want glued together. Likewise, place cardboard or paper between the garment you are gluing and the work surface, to prevent the glue from leaking through and adhering your garment to the surface.
7. Allow glue to dry before stitching over it, or the wet glue will clog your sewing machine (or hand-sewing needle and thread).

Sewing Shortcuts

We've discovered some sewing shortcuts along the way that we'd like to share with you. These shortcuts make applications easier, and often cut down on the number of steps you need to take in the application.

SEWING SHORTCUTS USING FABRIC GLUE

Denim can be a thick fabric, and sometimes using pins to hold layers together before stitching can be cumbersome (and pins can break a lot of sewing machine needles, too). Fabric glue is a great alternative way to hold denim layers together before you stitch them. We particularly recommend using fabric glue when working with heavyweight denims. (We always use Aleene's Fabric Glue because it adheres well without being too stiff when it dries.) Fabric glue also adds sturdiness to your deconstructed denim.

GLUING SHORTCUTS FOR SEAMS: Instead of pinning pieces together before stitching seams, secure them with fabric glue. Place a thin line of fabric glue on the right side of the fabric, close to raw edge of each piece. Matching raw edges, place pieces with right sides facing and press the layers together using your fingers. When glue dries, stitch ½-inch seam.

GLUING SHORTCUTS FOR APPLIQUÉS: Run a thin line of glue on the wrong side of appliqué, ⅛ to 1/16 inch from the raw edges of appliqué. Position appliqué on garment, and secure by pressing with fingers along edges. When glue is dry, topstitch (or hand stitch) around all edges.

GLUING SHORTCUTS FOR POCKETS, PLACKETS, ETC.: As with the appliqué, run a thin line of glue on wrong side of pocket, ⅛ to ¼ inch from raw or folded edge (depending on the pocket style). Position pocket on garment and secure by pressing with fingers along edges. When glue is dry, topstitch (or hand stitch) around all edges.

GLUING SHORTCUTS FOR HEMS: See page 33.

SEWING SHORTCUTS USING IRON-ON HEMMING TAPE

Iron-on hemming tape is a ½-inch strip of fabric that is dry-heat fusible on both sides, which makes it ideal for quick, sew-free hemming (see page 33). But, this quality also makes iron-on hemming tape an ideal shortcut for other sewing and garment construction tasks. Use it in place of pins, glue, or basting stitches. It will save you time (and some broken sewing machine needles).

IRON-ON HEMMING TAPE SHORTCUT FOR FABRIC LAYERS: When working with lightweight denim, you can use hemming tape, rather than straight pins, to baste the layers together before stitching. Cut hemming tape to same length as seam and sandwich it between the two fabric layers (with right sides facing), close to the raw edges. Fuse layers using a hot, dry iron, then stitch seam.

IRON-ON HEMMING TAPE SHORTCUT FOR ADHERING POCKETS, APPLIQUÉS, ETC.: As an alternative to glue, pinning, or hand or machine basting, you can secure appliqués, pockets, flaps, and other adornments with hemming tape. Cut appropriate length(s) of hemming tape. Position embellishment (pocket, appliqué, etc.) on garment and sandwich tape between wrong side of the embellishment and right side of the garment. Fuse together using a hot, dry iron; then hand or machine stitch around edges of embellishment.

IRON-ON HEMMING TAPE SHORTCUT FOR AP-PLYING BIAS BINDING: This is one of our favorite shortcuts because applying bias binding is a time-consuming process. Bias binding is used to finish raw edges in garment construction (such as hems and seams) and design details (such as pockets, flaps, lapels, and collars). Applying bias binding requires a two-step sewing process: first, you stitch it to the right side of the fabric, close to the edge it will cover; then, you fold it over that edge and stitch it again from the wrong side of the fabric. We use iron-on hemming tape to eliminate the first round of sewing. Cut bias binding (either single-fold or double-fold) and hemming tape the length of the edge to be covered (plus ½ inch extra on the bias binding so you can turn under the raw edges at each end). On ironing board, open bias binding and lay it flat, with the wrong side of the bias tape facing up. Lay hemming tape on top of bias binding, centering it over the fold (or center) of binding. Wrap bias binding/hem tape combo around raw edge, so an equal amount of bias binding is on right and wrong side of edge. Using a hot, dry iron, press over bias binding/hemming tape/fabric layers to fuse bias binding to garment edge. On sewing machine, you can now stitch through all layers, close to top folded edge of bias binding, for additional reinforcement. (See page 84 for illustrations of how to apply bias binding using iron-on hemming tape.)

Preparing Denim Garments

Depending on the type of denim you are deconstructing, it requires different preparation methods before transforming.

New Denim

New denim is often stiff and holds sizing. New denim, no matter what factory wash or finish, is stiffer than either vintage or prewashed denim, but it is not as stiff or hard as raw denim. To make it softer and easier to work with, turn new denim garments inside out and wash in cold water once or twice, and tumble dry at a high/hot setting. (If you do not want any shrinkage, dry with low heat or line dry.)

Raw Denim

Raw denim is a very stiff, hard fabric. To make it softer and easier to work with, turn raw denim garments inside out and wash in cold water at least three times, then place in the dryer and tumble dry at a high/hot setting to break down fibers and soften the raw denim more. (If you do not want any shrinkage, line dry.) Raw denim has not been pretreated. It is not distressed, washed, or broken down in any manner. Raw denim usually retains its hard, stiff look and feel until it has been washed many times.

Vintage denim is such a great texture to work with because it has basically been broken down already. Depending on where you retrieved your vintage denim, it is totally up to you if you wish to wash before or after sewing. We recommend washing your vintage denim on a delicate cycle, inside out, in cold water. Tumble dry or line dry to avoid any shrinkage. If you prefer the completely deconstructed look, then throw it in the dryer. It will shred the hemlines more.

Deconstructing Extra Denim Layers

When working on denim projects, it is crucial to get rid of extra layers of fabrics from seams, pockets, hems, collars, waistbands, and button and zipper plackets of the original jeans or jackets. We call the process of eliminating extra denim layers *deconstruction*. Denim fabric is very thick, and if you have too many layers it can be extremely difficult, or even impossible, so machine stitch or sew by hand. You also run the risk of snapping sewing machine needles.

Here are the places where deconstruction of extra denim layers may be required before you begin marking, cutting out, and sewing. You will use the same deconstruction techniques for all of the following:

Pants	Jackets and Shirts
Waistband (if you are detaching it)	Seams inside collar and collar stands
Zipper placket	Front button placket
Seams (side seams, inseams, front and back crotch seams)	Side seams
	Waistband (if you are detaching it)
Pockets	Pockets
	Cuffs

How to Deconstruct

1. Once you have cut your basic denim pieces (but before you mark them), use the seam ripper to remove the original topstitching on the top layer of your newly cut piece.

2. When the topstitching is completely removed, open the piece up and, using a small embroidery scissor, cut away any extra inside layers of denim you find—i.e., any denim layers sandwiched between the two outer layers. Depending on the original garment, you might have from two to four layers of denim sandwiched between the outer layers. It is crucial to remove all of those extra, inner layers.

3. Once you have removed those extra, inner layers, the outside top and bottom layers of the precut piece are intact, and you can start marking, cutting, and sewing.

shirts and tops

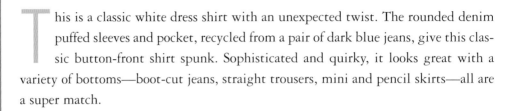

puffed-sleeved shirt

REQUIRED TIME:
1½ TO 2 HOURS

Can you believe that this working-class material has defined the look of a nation? It's a wardrobe staple for every American, but the rest of the world has caught on.

— Edward Norman

This is a classic white dress shirt with an unexpected twist. The rounded denim puffed sleeves and pocket, recycled from a pair of dark blue jeans, give this classic button-front shirt spunk. Sophisticated and quirky, it looks great with a variety of bottoms—boot-cut jeans, straight trousers, mini and pencil skirts—all are a super match.

In the time-honored tradition of respecting one's cloth, holding on to good fabric which still has life left in it, this double take on a favorite pair of jeans is fresh, sophisticated, and relevant. Whereas "recycling" of denim during the late 1960s turned your boyfriend's favorite jeans into your very own hippie skirt, twenty-first-century fashion imposes an expectation of polished worldliness on its clothing. This restyled shirt makes no apologies for its earlier lives, featuring a bone structure of outspoken exposed seams and voluptuously rounded fluted melon sleeves. Quite a second-take, and a new lease on life for a couple of old friends.

—Phyllis Magidson, costume curator for the Museum of the City of New York

Materials

STANDARD MATERIALS

Scissors

Marking devices

Heavy-duty straight pins

Aleene's Fabric Glue

Seam ripper

Measuring devices

Embroidery scissors

Sewing machine and sewing machine needles

Thread in matching or contrasting colors

Iron and ironing board

SPECIAL MATERIALS

Cotton, button-front dress shirt (men's or women's; one to two sizes larger than your size)

Pair of jeans, any size

Elastic, ¼ inch wide, 1 yard

Handsewing needle (heavy-duty/jeans weight)

Twill tape, ¼ inch wide, white or cream (to match shirt)

Pinking Shears

1. Using iron, carefully press shirt, flattening all seams. Lay shirt flat, right side out, front facing up. Mark new cutting lines on front and back of shirt, approximately ½ to 1 inch inside existing side and armhole seam lines, as shown. Using scissors, cut along dotted lines, as shown. Press.

2. Open shirt; lay it flat and right side out, as shown. If there is a box pleat at center back, press entire pleat perfectly flat, pin, then top-stitch along each side of pleat, ⅛ inch from folded edge, following stitching lines, as shown. Remove pins.

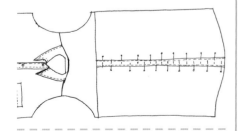

3. To mark new front and back side seams and bust darts, fold shirt in half lengthwise, right side out, and pin at center front, as shown. Using your body measurements (see page 26), mark cutting lines for side seams and bust dart, as shown. Cut along side-seam cutting lines. For dart, turn shirt inside out and mark dart fold line and stitching lines on wrong side of shirt.

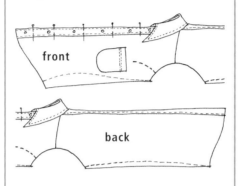

4. Remove one back pocket from jeans. Use seam ripper for about 1 inch, then switch to embroidery scissors to finish. Using scissors, trim excess denim from pocket, cutting between folded edge and topstitching, as shown. Press.

5. For sleeves, mark a rectangle (A), approximately 6 to 7 inches wide by 20 inches long, on one jean leg, as shown. Cut along marked lines, through both layers.

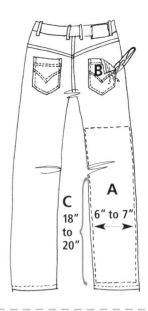

6. Fold each sleeve piece (A) in half width-wise, as shown; mark fold line, which is center of sleeve cap. Mark curved, sleeve-cap cutting line and underarm-seam cutting line, as shown below (see page 54). Pin layers together and cut along cutting lines through both layers, then open cut sleeves, as shown. Press.

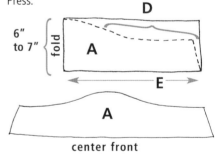

7. To sew bust dart, fold the front bodice along the dart fold line with right sides of shirt together, as shown. (You can cut along this fold line, if you prefer.) Pin. Using sewing machine, stitch dart, on *wrong* side of shirt, along dart stitching lines, as shown. Press bust darts. If you folded dart, press dart toward bottom of shirt; if you cut fold line of dart, press dart open and flat.

bust dart endpoints

8. With shirt right side up, place cutting board (or piece of cardboard or waxed paper) under whichever side of the shirt front has a pocket, and, inside pocket itself. Apply fabric glue to wrong side of denim pocket around all edges, and adhere denim pocket over original shirt pocket (see page 34). (If shirt has no pocket, center denim pocket beneath dart.) When glue is dry, machine stitch pocket to shirt front, about ⅛ inch from raw edges, leaving top edge of pocket free.

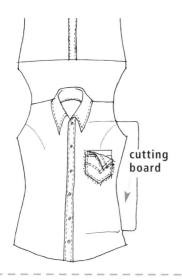

cutting board

9. Using tape measure, measure total length of front and back armholes. Gather sleeve caps by hand with a row of basting stitches 1 inch in from top outside edge of each sleeve cap. Remember we prefer to use a contrasting thread so that it is easier to remove after

sewing (see page 28). Pull thread from each end, gathering sleeve cap until it is the same length as total armhole measurement. Adjust gathers so they are evenly spaced, as shown; secure gathering threads at each end.

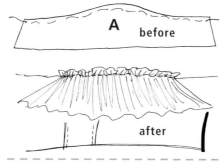

A before

after

10. Practice next step on scrap fabric first. Cut elastic to measure 2 inches less than the lower edge of the sleeve. Lay sleeve wrong side up and place elastic ½ inch in from bottom (ungathered) edge; position all layers under presser foot of sewing machine, as shown. Using a small, straight stitch, backstitch to secure elastic in place, then continue to stitch down the center of the elastic, stretching elastic slightly, and evenly, while stitching. (The sleeve will automatically gather.) Repeat on bottom edge of other sleeve.

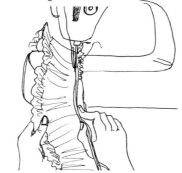

11. To attach sleeve, lay shirt flat, wrong side up, and position sleeve, right side up, on top of armhole opening (*wrong* sides of shirt and sleeve are together.) Pin baste sleeve into armhole, matching center of sleeve cap to

shoulder seam, easing gathers so sleeve fits armhole, as shown. (Raw edge of gathered sleeve will show on right side/outside of shirt.) Place twill tape on inside of sleeve over gathering stitches (1 inch from raw edge), then machine stitch sleeve to armhole through twill tape and both fabric layers, as shown.

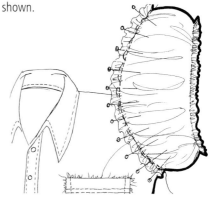

12. Turn shirt inside out. With right sides together, pin shirt fronts to shirt backs at side seams and sleeves, matching curved edges of sides and armhole seams. Place twill tape along seam lines of side seams only. Machine stitch ½-inch seams (through center of twill tape on side seams), as shown (see page 33). Press seams open and flat. Turn shirt right side out; press.

denim accents shirt

REQUIRED TIME:
1 ½ TO 2 HOURS

*Denim is one of
the world's oldest
fabrics, yet it
remains eternally
young.*

*— American Fabrics
Magazine,* 1969

Denim details gently light up this classic white shirt. The denim waistband, accompanied by a strip of deconstructed denim on the front pocket, and the left shoulder epaulet, made from an old jean zipper, quietly update this shirt. It can be worn as a lightweight jacket over soft cotton T-shirts or dainty camisoles. A great layering piece or on its own with pants or a skirt; it can be dressed up or down for easygoing chic.

Materials

STANDARD MATERIALS

Scissors

Marking devices

Heavy-duty straight pins

Aleene's Fabric Glue

Seam ripper

Measuring devices

Embroidery scissors

Sewing machine and sewing machine needles

Thread (to match or contrast with jeans)

Iron and ironing board

SPECIAL MATERIAL

Men's or women's cotton button-front dress shirt, with pocket

Men's jeans (waist on jeans should be the same measurement
   as your upper/high hip)

Twill tape, ¼ inch wide, white or cream (to match shirt)

1. Using iron, carefully press shirt, flattening all seams. Lay shirt flat, right side out, front facing up. Mark new cutting lines on front of shirt, approximately $\frac{1}{2}$ to 1 inch inside existing side and armhole seam lines, as shown. Using scissors, cut along dotted cutting lines, through both layers.

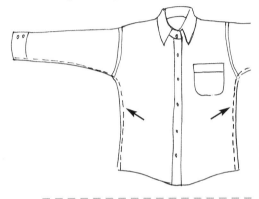

2. Fold collar up and carefully cut it off by cutting through the collar just above the stitched edge of the collar band, as shown. Press shirt again.

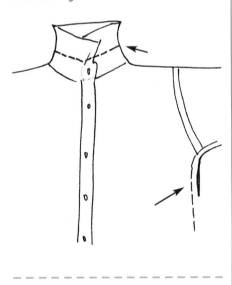

3. Open shirt right side out and lay it flat, right side up, on a table (*not* on the floor); fold in half down center front and center back, with sleeves extended out, as shown. Pin along center front, center back, and sides, as shown. Using your body measurements (see page 27), mark cutting lines for side seams, as shown. Cut along side seam cutting lines. Remove all pins.

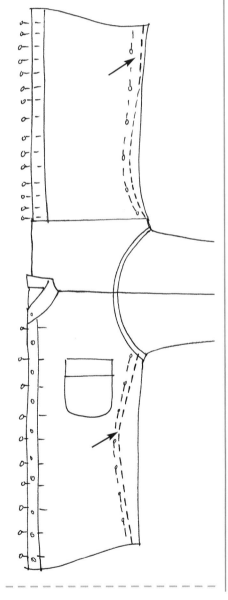

4. Fold shirt at shoulder seams, with *wrong* sides together, so raw edges of sleeves match; pin raw edges of sleeves, as shown. Mark new sleeve cutting lines (width and shape of sleeves per your taste), as shown (see page 27). Cut along cutting lines.

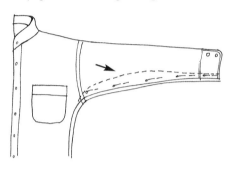

5. Using seam ripper, detach bottom of belt loops from jeans, leaving loops attached to top of waistband. Cut waistband from jeans, just below seam line, as shown. When band is cut off, the belt loops will extend past waistband. (Note: Be sure waist measurement of jeans equals your upper/high hip measurement.) For denim pocket flap, cut rectangle 2 inches high and same width as top of shirt pocket, as shown.

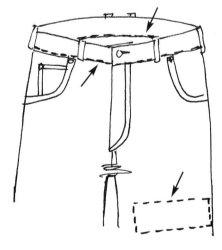

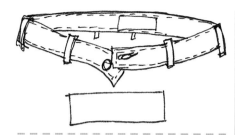

6. Using seam ripper or embroidery scissors, completely remove zipper from zipper placket of jeans, as shown. Once zipper is removed, trim all of the excess denim from top part of the zipper and leave just ¼ inch of denim on the zipper, following dotted lines as shown in Detail B. Close zipper and pull zipper tab completely off zipper, as shown in Detail C.

7. With shirt right side out, position trimmed zipper at top front shoulder, as shown, and glue in place with fabric glue. (Remember to put something between shirt and table surface to prevent glue leakage.) Machine stitch zipper to shirt, close to raw edges of zipper, following stitching lines, as shown. Place denim pocket flap along top of shirt pocket and glue in place. When glue dries, machine stitch side edges of pocket flap, following seam lines of pocket, leaving top edge of pocket free. Cut shirttails off shirt so bottom edge is straight, as shown.

NOTE: You can also add a decorative topstitch in a contrasting color around the armhole, as shown, for extra drama.

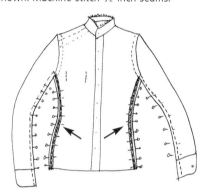

8. Turn shirt inside out. Position twill tape on the side seams only (see page 33), then pin side seams and underarm seams together, matching curves and armhole seams, as shown. Machine stitch ½-inch seams.

9. To attach denim waistband to bottom of shirt, first glue wrong side of waistband to right side of shirt; when glue dries, topstitch waistband to shirt, ⅛ inch from edge of band, following dotted lines, as shown.

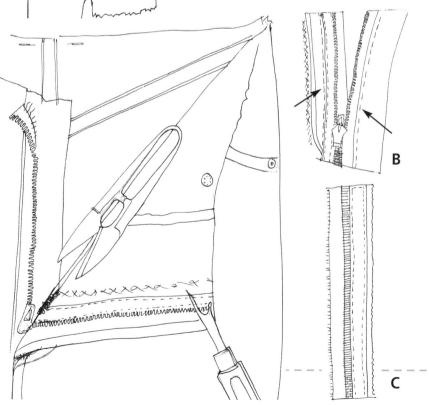

B

C

bow-tied halter top

REQUIRED TIME:

1 HOUR

If we were to use a human term to describe a textile we might say that denim is an honest fabric—substantial, forthright, and unpretentious.

— *American Fabrics Magazine*, 1962

Constructed from a colorful T-shirt attached to the cut-off waistband from a pair of dark blue vintage jeans, this top is an outright showstopper. The extremely long neck sash allows for various tying options. The blouson halter style can be worn with many different types of bottoms—long, flowing skirts, boot-cut jeans, or culottes. We suggest covering your legs, since your entire back is revealed.

This project is not only about the denim but the T-shirt as well—we recommend using a T-shirt with elaborate silk screening. Here we chose a royal blue T-shirt with a beautifully screened image of a Native American and an eagle, which complements the dark blue denim used at the waist.

A die-hard supporter of Sistahs of Harlem, Fatima Robinson, choreographer-dancer-director extraordinaire, has sported our threads since the inception of the company. "I love the this halter top because it is versatile, free, and moving."

Materials

STANDARD MATERIALS

Scissors

Marking devices

Heavy-duty straight pins

Aleene's Fabric Glue

Seam ripper

Measuring devices

Embroidery scissors

Thread (to match or contrast)

Sewing machine and sewing machine needles

Iron and ironing board

SPECIAL MATERIALS

1 L or XL T-shirt, your choice of color and print

1 pair of jeans, well fitting or one size smaller (dark denim suggested)

Masking tape

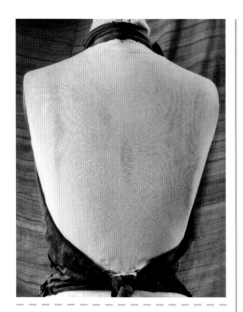

1. Using iron, press T-shirt right side out, completely flat.

2. Fold T-shirt, right side out, in half along center front, as shown; lay flat. Mark new cutting lines around neck, shoulders, and sleeve, as shown. For neck, mark line starting at shoulder seam, 1 inch out from neck band, and ending about 1/2 inch below neckband at center front. For new armhole, start at same shoulder seam point as new neck cutting line, ending at a point about 4 inches below underarm. Using masking tape, label this piece A, as shown; it is the top of the halter.

Mark three horizontal cutting lines on body of shirt—one 14 inches down from shoulder seam, the next 6 inches below the first line, and the last 4 inches below the second line, as shown. Using masking tape, label pieces B–D, as shown. (B and C will become waistband and tie; D will become neck band and tie.) On sleeve, mark cutting line about 1 inch outside armhole seam, as shown in red; label this E.

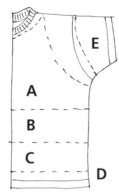

3. Using scissors, cut through both layers, following cutting lines, as marked. On halter piece (A), cut the front away from the back at side seams, and keep piece cut from shirt front only, as shown below. Cut away side seams on pieces B and C, then stitch them together at one short end to create one long piece, as shown. Cut away one side seam on

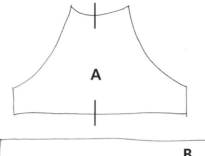

piece D and lay flat, as shown. Mark center front at top and bottom of halter piece (A).

4. Take one piece E (formerly a sleeve) and cut it down the center, as shown, saving both pieces for later. (Pin them together so they don't get misplaced.)

5. Cut away a section of the front of jeans only, just inside the side seams and about 4 to 5 inches down from the waistband, following cutting lines, as shown. Using a seam ripper and embroidery scissors, remove zipper from precut jean front (see page 47, Step 6). Now, remove all the extra layers of fabric from the jean waist band (see page 37).

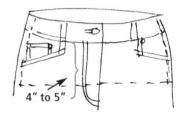

6. On piece A, gather neck and bottom edges by hand or machine stitching a row of basting stitches 1 inch down from top of neckline, and at bottom, 1 inch up from raw edge, as shown. Pull basting threads from both ends in a drawstring motion, until the top edge is the same measurement as your front neck and the bottom edge the same measurement as your front waist, as shown (see page 29).

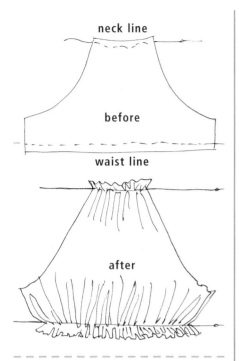

neck line

before

waist line

after

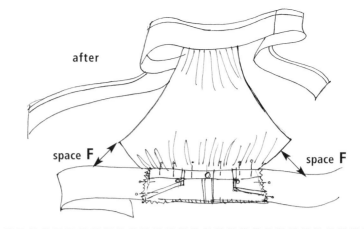

after

space **F**

space **F**

7. Take neck band/tie piece D and, with right sides together, pin piece D to gathered neck-line of halter piece A, matching raw edges and center of D to center of A, as shown.

With right sides together, pin waist-band/tie piece B/C to bottom of piece A, matching raw edges and center seam of B/C to center of bottom edge of A. Stitch neck band/tie (D) to neck of halter (A), and waist-band/tie (B/C) to bottom of halter (A) with a ¼-inch seam, following dotted lines as shown.

On right side, press neck band up over neck seam, and bottom band down over bottom seam.

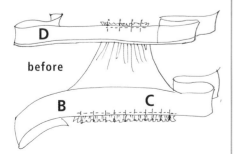

D

before

B   C

8. Take precut jean front (from Step 5) and pin or glue the *wrong* side of the jean front waistband over right side of the waistband/tie (B/C), matching top edge of jean front to top edge of band, and zipper placket of jean front to center front of band, as shown. With the right side facing up, place all layers under presser foot of sewing machine and stitch jean front to shirt front about ¼ inch from top edge of jean waistband, and again ¼ inch from bottom edge of waistband. Press seams flat.

Note spaces marked F on illustration; these are important for next step.

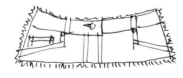

9. Now use the two precut E pieces to fill the gaps between the sides of the halter top and the waistband/ties (this gap is labeled F in previous illustration). Mark cut lines in the shape of a triangle on the two E pieces, as shown. The shortest edge of the triangle should be the same length as the raw, side edge of the halter (labeled G in illustration), and the other two sides of triangle should be about 7 inches long. Right sides together, pin triangle pieces to halter and waistband/ties,

with the shortest side of triangle pinned to halter top, and one long edge of triangle pinned to waistband/tie, as shown. Stitch tri-angles in place, as shown. Press seams flat.

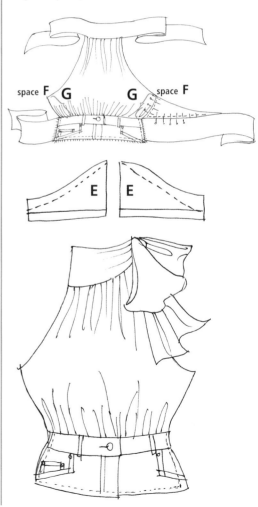

space **F**   **G**   **G**   space **F**

E   E

ruffled t-shirt top

REQUIRED TIME:
45 MINUTES USING
SEWING MACHINE

1 ½ HOURS BY
HAND

*Where's my jeans?...
I need a butt lift
without the surgery!*

— Jackie Stone,
   filmmaker,
   getting dressed for
   a night on the town

A simple T-shirt turns fabulous with denim appliqués and an added waistband detail at bottom edge. The ultrafeminine ruffles and denim appliqués are delightful and flirty. The beauty of this style is its simplicity. You need only the bare essentials—a solid-colored T-shirt and a few denim scraps. It can be also be worn with trousers or a pencil skirt for an upscale casual flair.

We all have days where we must transform our day looks to night looks in five minutes or less. As a result, our customers love our transitional garments that can move freely from one atmosphere to another. Life happens as we go unexpected places. But, of course, we want you to be dressed appropriately—and this top helps you to be just that.

Materials

STANDARD MATERIALS

Scissors

Marking devices

Heavy-duty straight pins

Aleene's Fabric Glue

Seam ripper

Measuring devices

Embroidery scissors

Thread in matching or contrasting colors

Sewing machine and sewing machine needles

Iron and ironing board

SPECIAL MATERIALS

M or L T-shirt, just slightly larger than your correct size and depending on how tight you want the T-shirt to be

Large scaps of different shades of denim and a front waistband

Twill tape, ¼ inch wide (color to match T-shirt)

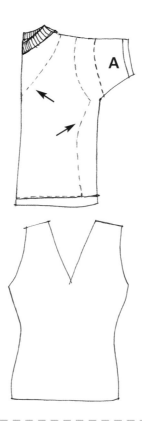

1. Using iron, press T-shirt perfectly flat. Fold T-shirt in half right side out, along center front, as shown. Mark new cutting lines on shirt, as shown, using your measurements to determine cutting lines (see page 24).

For new neckline cutting line, measure out on shoulder seam about 1 inch from neck band and draw a diagonal line to center front of T-shirt, about 6 inches down from neck band, as shown. Begin new armhole cut line at shoulder seam, 2 to 3 inches out from neck cutting line, following curve of armhole, ending about 1 inch in from underarm, as shown.

Using body measurements, mark new side seam, then mark a horizontal line about 1 inch up from bottom, as shown.

Next, mark cutting line on sleeve, about 1 to 2 inches from armhole, following curve of armhole on T-shirt, to create piece A, as shown.

Using scissors, cut along all dotted lines, through both layers. DO NOT CUT shoulder seams. Unfold cut T-shirt, press, and set to the side.

2. Take each piece A (cut from T-shirt sleeves), cut away seam, lay flat, and press. Hand or machine baste 1 inch down from top (curved) edge of each piece A, as shown. Pull thread from both ends to gather pieces into ruffles, as shown (see page 29). These ruffled pieces will be sleeves, and each should be the same length as the total armhole measurement.

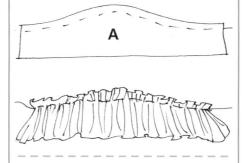

3. For leaf appliqués, cut 2 square denim pieces from jeans leg, as shown, anywhere from 4 inches by 4 inches to 6 inches by 6 inches, depending on how dramatic you want appliqués to be. We suggest you use a couple different colors of denim, so you can cut from two different pairs of jeans, or use large scraps from previous projects.

Cut away the *front* waistband *only* from jeans, as shown. Deconstruct extra denim layers from waistband (see page 37).

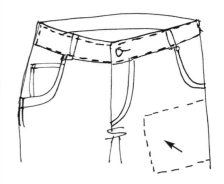

4. Using chalk, pencil, or pen, draw 3 to 4 leaf shapes on *wrong* side of denim squares, as shown below. Cut out leaf shapes. Press as necessary.

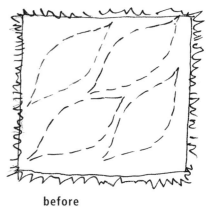

before

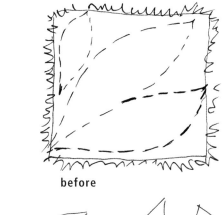

before

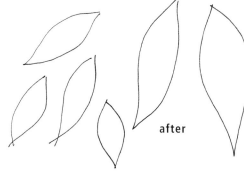

after

5. Open T-shirt and lay flat, as shown. Place appliqués anywhere you like on front of shirt, then glue them in place (see page 34).

Glue front waistband from jeans to bottom of T-shirt front, matching raw edge of T-shirt to bottom edge of waistband. Cut waistband so it is $1/2$ inch shorter than T-shirt at each side seam. (This will make sewing the $1/2$-inch side seams, which you'll do later, much easier.) If you wish, you can topstitch waistband to shirt front after glue dries.

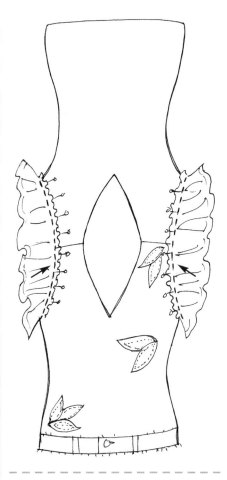

6. Pin *wrong* side of ruffled sleeve to *right* side of armhole, with raw edge of gathered sleeve overlapping raw edge of armhole by about $1 1/4$ inches. Stitch sleeve to armhole along gathered basting line, about 1 inch from raw edge of gathered sleeve, making sure stitching is going through both sleeve and armhole layers. Press seam. (Raw edge of gathered sleeve will be visible on right side of

shirt, as shown.) Turn garment inside out and, right sides together, matching front to back at side seams and sleeves; pin. Place twill tape along stitching lines of side seams (see page 33), as shown. Stitch $1/2$-inch seams, as shown. Turn right side out, and press.

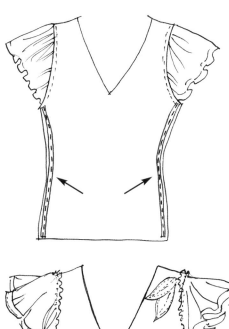

boat-neck pullover

REQUIRED TIME:
35 MINUTES

They transcend fashion, income, and social barriers, enjoy universal appeal, and have been wardrobe staples for nearly half a century now. No doubt, if asked to select the apparel equivalent of "Desert Island Discs," most people would number their favorite pair of jeans among the must-have clothing they would want to be marooned on a desert island with.

— www.arvindmills.com /Fabrics/denim.html

A deconstructed sweatshirt has large-scale appliqués at the top created from various shades of denim and black leather. Finished with a grosgrain ribbon drawstring at the lower edge, this top is a lounger's delight. It's an updated '80s throwback and a tribute to all dancers—a reminder of the years when we sliced the collars off our sweatshirts, mesmerized by Alex Owens (played by Jennifer Beals) as she resiliently pursued her dancing ambitions in the movie *Flashdance*. We loved the comfort and sensuality of her hard-core workouts, and the way she always managed to look fresh.

A perfect cover-up to wear over a leotard or leggings before yoga class or on the weekend paired with a high-heeled boot for easy chic. It's supremely comfortable without compromising your style. Not to mention, a cinch to make.

Materials

STANDARD MATERIALS

Scissors

Marking devices

Heavy-duty straight pins

Aleene's Fabric Glue

Seam ripper

Measuring devices

Embroidery scissors

Thread in matching or contrasting color

Sewing machine and sewing machine needles

Iron and ironing board

SPECIAL MATERIALS

L to LX sweatshirt, depending on how loose you want top
   (color of your choice)

Scraps of leather, from shoe stores, leather stores, fabric stores,
   or old gloves, or, soft, pliable leather belts

Scraps of denim, from a pair of jeans or skirt, or, from previous projects

Ribbon, rat-tail cord, or the inside seam of a pair of jeans

Twill tape, ¼ inch wide, (to match sweatshirt)

Large safety pin

1. Using iron, press sweatshirt. Turn sweatshirt inside out and fold it in half along center front, as shown. Mark curved cutting line on sweatshirt front for boat neck, from approximately 2 inches out from neck band at shoulder seam, to about 1 inch down from neck band at center front, as shown. Using scissors, cut boat neck, following cutting lines.

2. Keep sweatshirt inside out and flat. Mark new cutting line on sleeve, from cuff to about 1 inch under armhole (line D, as shown). Mark another cutting line on side seam, from waistband up about 2½ inches, and another cutting line across front, just above waistband, as shown. (Note: Do *not* cut side seams of sweatshirt except for 1 inch under armhole and 2½ inches above waistband.) Repeat on other side.

With sweatshirt still inside out and right sides together, match raw edges of sleeve fronts to sleeve backs (line D); pin, and stitch ½-inch seams. Turn right side out. Press seams.

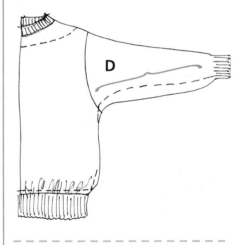

3. Using any scraps of denim or leather you like, draw, cut out, and attach appliqués, as shown (see pages 54 and 55, Steps 3, 4, and 5).

Turn sweatshirt inside out. Fold bottom of shirt up 2½ inches, pin in place, then stitch through all layers following stitching line, as shown, creating casing for drawstring.

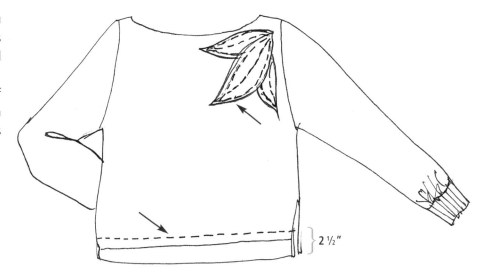

2½"

4. Turn sweatshirt right side out. Press. From cord, ribbon, or long pieces of seam cut from denim jeans, make a drawstring about 36 inches longer than bottom circumference of shirt. Put a safety pin through one end of the drawstring, insert it in casing, and pull drawstring through entire length of tunnel and out the other end, holding on to safety pin as you pull it through. Knot each end of the drawstring, as shown.

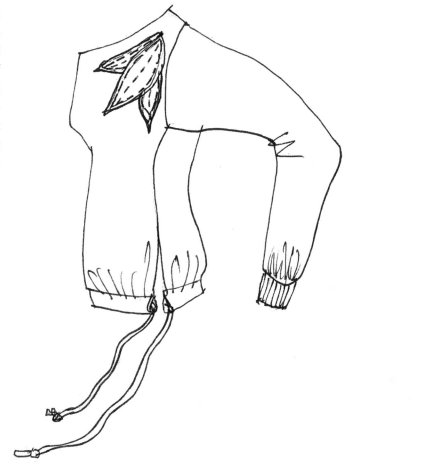

v-neck shirt with crossover collar

REQUIRED TIME:

1½ HOURS

Denim does seem to endure. It looks good on masses of body types and skin tones. People wear it in the summer and the winter. And in the past couple of years, denim has made the leap from trips to the grocery store to elegant settings that once required skirts and ties.

— Teresa F. Lindeman, "Clothing: Retailers Place Bet on Jeans," *Pittsburgh Post-Gazette*, August 21, 2005

A fashion-forward creation that will stand the test of time—this shirt is a surprisingly complementary combination of galleria and punk. A basic white dress shirt is deconstructed, the sleeves are removed and the front cut into a low V-neck, side seams are reshaped and the lower edge pinked. Denim details are added—an unusual but smart crossover collar, a back pocket stitched to the front of the shirt, and a patch applied at one shoulder. It all adds up to one smart-looking top that can be worn year round.

Materials

STANDARD MATERIALS

Scissors

Marking devices

Heavy-duty straight pins

Aleene's Fabric Glue

Seam ripper

Measuring devices

Embroidery scissors

Thread in matching or contrasting colors

Sewing machine and sewing machine needles

Iron and ironing board

SPECIAL MATERIALS

1 men's dress shirt or women's dress shirt (cotton)

1 pair of jeans, any size

Twill tape, ¼ inch wide, white or cream (color to match shirt)

Snaps for denim (Note: Shoe repair shops carry these snaps, and will attach them to your garment.)

Tracing paper (any type of paper thin enough to see through)

Pinking shears

1. Using iron, carefully press shirt, flattening all seams. Lay shirt flat, right side out, front facing up. Mark new cutting lines on front of shirt, approximately $\frac{1}{2}$ to 1 inch inside existing side and armhole seam lines, as shown below. Using scissors, cut along new cutting lines, through both layers. Turn collar up and carefully cut it off by cutting through the collar just above the stitched edge of the collar stand, as shown on page 46. Cut off bottom of shirt, in a slightly curved line, at about hipbone level, as shown, with pinking shears.

2. Mark cutting lines for strip A (which will be the new collar) and rectangle C (which will be shoulder overlay/appliqué) on one jean leg, as shown. Strip A should be 24 inches by 2 inches; rectangle C, $4\frac{1}{2}$ inches by 5 inches. (Note: You will sew piece C to the shirt before stitching side seams.)

Using seam ripper and embroidery scissors, remove back pocket from jeans and trim extra fabric layers; as shown in pocket detail A (see page 37). Mark new stitching lines on trimmed pocket, as shown in pocket detail B.

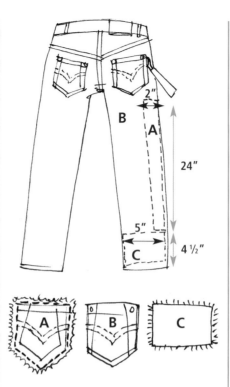

3. If using a women's dress shirt, you can skip this step. If using a men's dress shirt, you'll want to make bust darts on the shirt front, as shown. Using body measurements, mark bust darts on wrong side of shirt, as shown (see page 24). With right sides facing, fold along dart fold line, and stitch along dart stitching lines, as shown with dotted line (see page 42, Step 7).

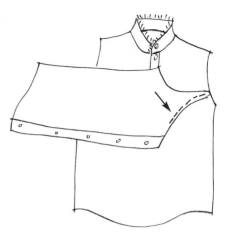

4. Fold collar piece A in half, as shown. Using scissors, trim open ends (not folded end) to a curve or a point, as shown below. Put collar to the side until needed for Step 10.

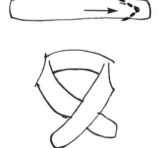

5. Open shirt right side out and fold in half at center front, lay flat, and pin, as shown. Place tracing paper over right shoulder of shirt, as shown. Trace your desired shape for the shoulder overlay/appliqué, and cut out along cutting lines. This is your shoulder overlay/appliqué pattern. Draw a line down the center of pattern, as shown.

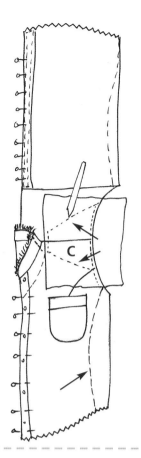

6. Trace paper pattern made in Step 5 onto denim piece C. (Be sure to trace center line.) Cut out along *outside* cutting lines only, as shown. Topstitch $\frac{1}{8}$ to $\frac{1}{4}$ inch from all raw edges, as shown.

7. Refer to illustration above (Step 5) and mark cutting line to cut off *front* collar stand (*not* back of stand) and top of shirt, as shown with dotted lines. Cut off front only.

Using body measurements, mark new side seams on shirt front, as shown (see page 24).

Cut along all cutting lines, through both layers.

On back of shirt, press, pin, and topstitch center back pleat (see page 42, Step 2). Using body measurements, mark side seam cutting lines on shirt back; cut along new cutting lines, through both layers.

8. Using fabric glue, glue shoulder overlay/appliqué to front and back shoulder of shirt, matching center of C to shoulder seam, as shown (see page 34).

Glue pocket to pocket of shirt. When glue dries, unbutton shirt and, on right side, sew denim to shirt at shoulder and pocket, following lines, as shown. Be sure to leave top of pocket free, and sew only through front layer of shirt.

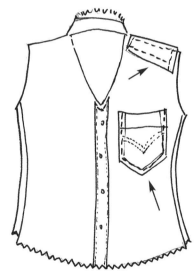

9. Turn shirt inside out, with right sides together, pin shirt front to shirt back at side seams, matching curves. Stitch side seams in $\frac{1}{2}$-inch seam, using twill tape, as shown (see page 33).

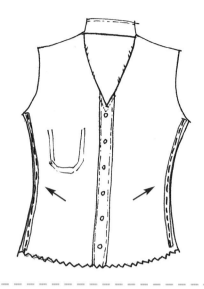

10. Take collar piece (A), and topstitch about $\frac{1}{8}$ inch from all edges. With wrong side of collar facing right side of shirt, pin collar to top edge of collar stand, starting at center back of neckband. Stitch collar to back collar stand, stitching over collar's topstitching, as shown below. Add heavy-duty denim snap to ends of collar, following instructions on purchased snap packaging, or, have it attached at a shoe repair shop. Place snap so collar snaps comfortably at front of neck.

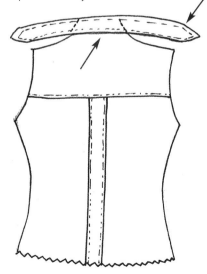

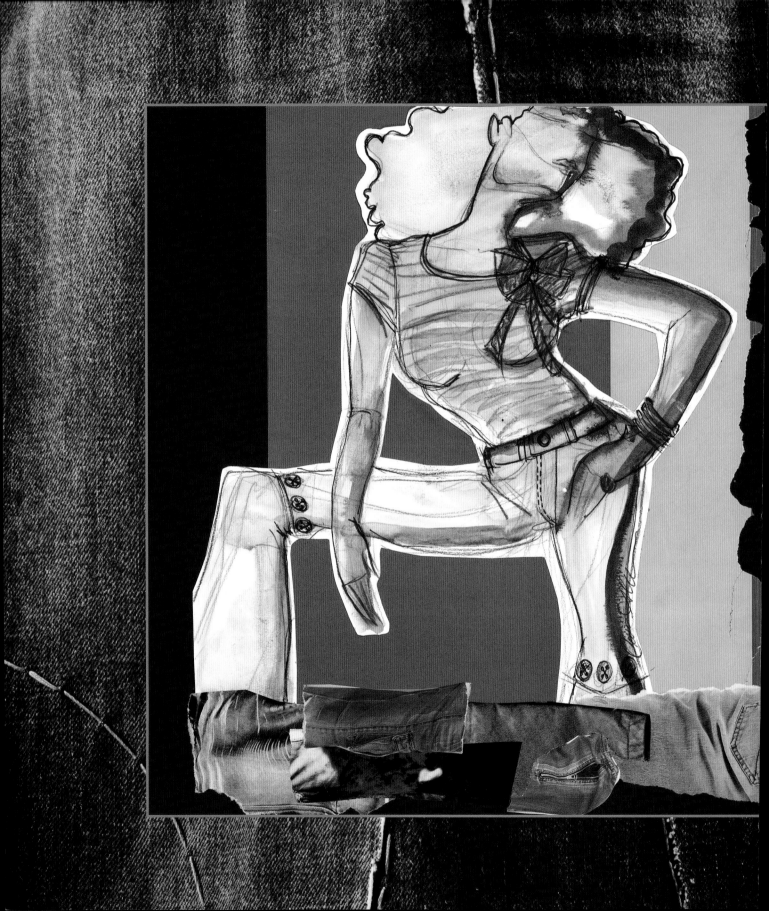

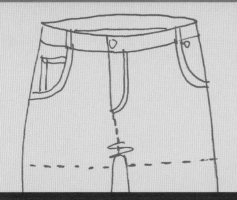
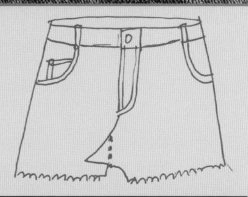

skirts and bottoms

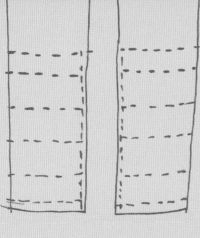
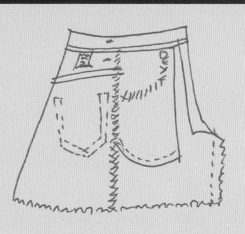
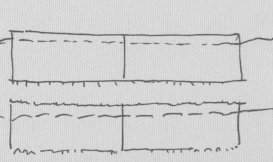
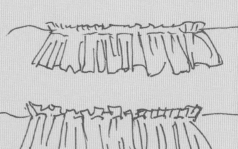

skirt with pickstitched details

REQUIRED TIME:
45 MINUTES

My jeans and I have chemistry. They mold to my body without me asking.

— Soho shopper in New York City

This garment is made from a pair of vintage jeans converted into an A-line skirt. Our pattern is finished with embroidery-floss topstitching, but the skirt can be finished with any technique from pages 12–15. A knee-length A-line skirt is always popular. It flatters most figures. It's effortlessly sexy.

This skirt can save a dated pair of pants from the garbage. It looks awesome with an array of tops: long sleeved; short sleeved V-, U-, and crewnecks, those with a fitted bodice, or flowing baby-doll tops.

Materials

STANDARD MATERIALS

Scissors

Marking devices

Aleene's Fabric Glue

Seam ripper

Measuring devices

Embroidery scissors

Sewing machine and sewing machine needles

Thread in matching or contrasting color

SPECIAL MATERIALS

1 pair of well-fitting jeans

Twill tape ¼" wide (color to match skirt)

Embroidery floss (any color you choose; we chose metallic colors)

Thimble

Embroidery needles

NOTE: DO NOT USE HEAVY-DUTY STRAIGHT PINS ON THIS PROJECT.

The layers of denim are thick at the crotch areas, and you don't want to damage your sewing machine.

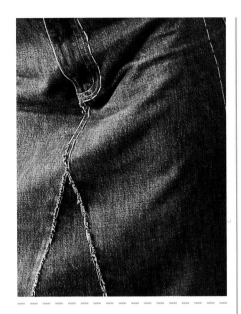

1. Lay jeans flat, right side out and front side up. Mark cutting lines on front of each lower leg, as shown. Piece A should be 8 inches by

15 inches; piece B should be 8 inches by 15 inches. Using scissors, cut out piece A, through front leg layer *only*, following cutting lines. Cut out piece B, through *both* front and back layers, following cutting lines, *leaving outside leg seam intact.*

- -

2. Using scissors, cut bottoms of jeans legs, through both layers, so they are even. Length should equal desired finished length of skirt.

Using seam ripper or embroidery scissors, rip out crotch seams and inside leg seams of jeans, on both front and back of jeans. Deconstruct extra denim layers from front and back crotch and inside leg seams (see page 37). On front of jeans, with jeans right side out and front side up, overlap crotch "triangle" from left side of jeans over crotch triangle on right side of jeans, as shown. Overlap so that all layers lay flat and smooth; glue in place with fabric glue (see page 34). Repeat crotch triangle procedure on back of jeans. When glue is dry, topstitch, 1/8 inch from raw edges of crotch triangles, through both layers, on both front and back.

With jeans right side out and front facing up, take piece A (cut in Step 1) and place it under the open space between the two front jeans legs, making sure all layers lay flat and smooth. Glue in place. (See page 34.) When glue is dry, topstitch through all layers, 1/8 inch from raw edges of inside leg seams. Trim off excess material on inside of triangles.

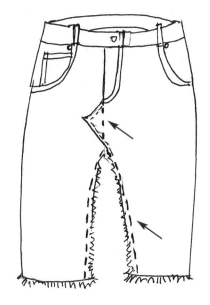

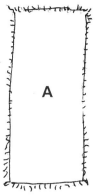

3. Lay jeans flat, right side out, with back of jeans facing up. At top of back, mark cutting lines in an inverted triangle shape, beginning at waistband and continuing diagonally down to a point about 1/2 inch below center back yoke, as shown. Slide the two cut edges together so they overlap, and glue. Once glue is dry, topstitch together.

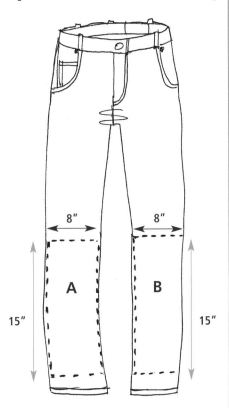

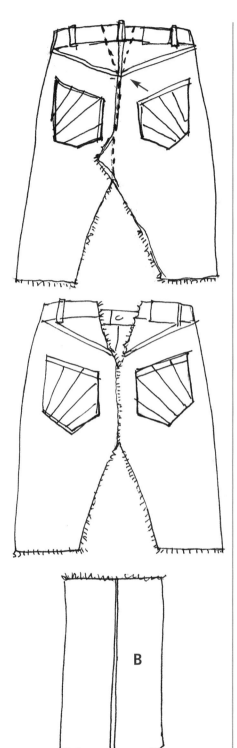

4. Lay piece B flat. As you did on front of skirt, with skirt right side out and back of skirt facing up, place B under open leg seams of skirt back, making sure all layers lay flat and smooth. Glue in place. When glue is dry, top-stitch through all layers, ⅛ inch from raw edges. Trim inside.

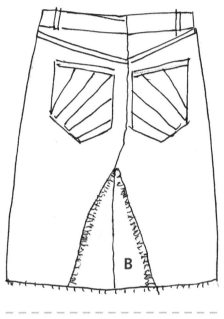

5. Skirt is now fully assembled. Using embroidery floss of your choice, decorate front and back of skirt around triangle insets and down sides with pickstitches, or other stitches of your choice.

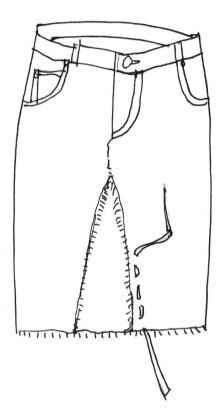

ribbon-trim miniskirt

REQUIRED TIME:
40 MINUTES

A simple fabric, dating back to seventeenth-century France, it has become an instant sign of credibility and sex appeal.

— *Denim from Cowboys to Catwalks: A History of the World's Most Legendary Fabric* by Graham Marsh and Paul Trynka

V intage jeans are transformed into a deconstructed miniskirt with a contrasting patterned ribbon woven through slits at the lower edge. This saucy skirt is best appreciated in warmer climates. However, you can always add a pair of tights or legwarmers for additional warmth. And the ribbon can be easily changed for a different look—strips of leather, grosgrain ribbon, silk satin, organza—all will work.

This is the perfect skirt for daring denim lovers who desire to flaunt their legs. The spinning classes pay off when wearing this skirt. We can all learn from Tina Turner—who wasn't afraid to flaunt those iconic limbs well into her forties, fifties, sixties . . .

Materials

STANDARD MATERIALS

Scissors

Marking devices

Aleene's Fabric Glue

Seam ripper

Heavy-duty straight pins

Measuring devices

Embroidery scissors

Sewing machine and sewing machine needles

Thread in matching or contrasting colors

Iron and ironing board

SPECIAL MATERIALS

1 pair of jeans that fit well

Embroidery needle

Embroidery floss

Fusible interfacing

Ribbon, 3 yards (fabric, color, and width of ribbon is your choice)

NOTE: DO NOT USE HEAVY-DUTY STRAIGHT PINS EXCEPT ON STEP **4** OF THIS PROJECT.
The layers of denim are quite thick, and you don't want to damage your sewing machine.

1. Lay jeans flat, right side out and front side up. Mark horizontal cutting lines on front of each leg, 12 to 13 inches down from top of waistband, as shown. Using scissors, cut legs off along horizontal cutting lines, through both layers.

Using seam ripper or embroidery scissors, rip open inside leg seams and front and back crotch seams. Deconstruct extra denim layers from front and back crotch and inside leg seams (see page 37).

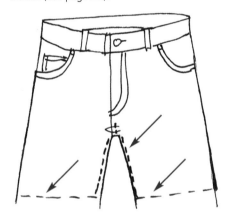

2. Lay jeans flat, right side out and front side up. Now, cut off both crotch triangles from front crotch of jeans *only*, as shown, leaving a $\frac{1}{2}$-inch seam allowance for seam you will sew in Step 4.

3. Turn jeans over, right side out, so back of jeans is facing up. Overlap crotch triangle from left side of jeans over crotch triangle on right side of jeans, making sure all layers lay flat and smooth, as shown; glue (see page 34). When glue is dry, topstitch through all layers, $\frac{1}{8}$ inch from raw edges of crotch "triangle." Backstitch over point of triangle.

Mark horizontal cutting line across entire back of jeans, at level of crotch point, as shown below. Cut along cutting lines, through both back and front of skirt. This is your new hemline.

4. Turn your miniskirt inside out. Place right sides of legs together at center front, matching raw edges, and pin, as shown. (This is the center front seam of the skirt.) Stitch with $\frac{1}{2}$-inch seam.

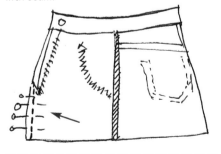

5. With skirt still inside out, use iron to press all seams perfectly flat, on both front and back.

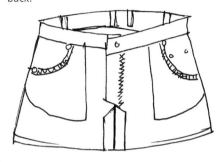

6. With skirt still inside out, turn it so the back is facing up. Glue insides of crotch triangle that are loose to the skirt back, as shown. (Remember to put something between the front and back of skirt so you do not glue them together, too.) Let glue dry.

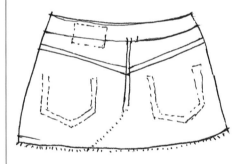

7. Turn skirt right side out. Stitch around bottom of skirt, about $\frac{1}{2}$ inch from raw edge, to create faux hem, as shown below.

8. Using clear gridded ruler and chalk or pencil that wipes or irons off, mark vertical lines about $3/4$ inch above faux hem stitching line, all around skirt, front and back. When cut, these lines will be the slits through which you lace your ribbon. The lines should be $1/8$ inch longer than the width of your ribbon; the distance between cut lines should alternate between $1^3/4$ inches and $2^3/4$ inches.

Cut a long strip of fusible interfacing the same length as the bottom circumference of your skirt and slightly wider than the slits.

Following manufacturer's directions, iron the interfacing to the wrong side of the skirt under the marked lines for the slits.

Cut marked slit lines.

Lace your ribbon through the slits, going under the space between the slits that are $1^3/4$ inches apart and over the slits that are $2^3/4$ inches apart. Tie ends of ribbon together into a knot or bow at side front of skirt, as shown in photograph.

drafting ruler

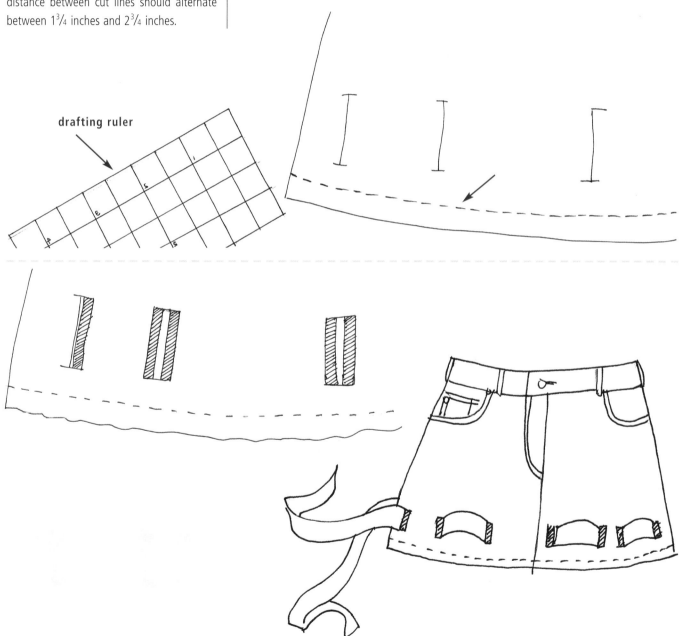

ruffled miniskirt

**REQUIRED TIME:
1 HOUR**

*Sexier than no
clothes at all, jeans
began to suggest
good times to a
whole generation.*

— Cotton Incorporated
Lifestyle Monitor,
Denim Issue,
March 30, 2006,
www.cottoninc.com.

A pair of perfectly faded and gently softened vintage jeans are transformed into a deconstructed miniskirt with random denim ruffles. Tantalizing and playful—a guaranteed party skirt. We layered the ruffles for flavor galore, but if the spice is too much, decrease the number. It's easy to make, fun to wear, and makes a definite fashion impact.

From Carmia: I wear our label often. With the hustle and bustle of New York, I'm always ready to glide in the direction that the city pulls me as an entrepreneur. I have to seize the moment when I have it. I'm heading to a business meeting with Carmen {the other Sistah of Harlem} to discuss the happenings of the week's work. Traffic light—red; it's one of the only reasons to stop walking in the city, unless you spot a precious dog or some fabulous threads to buy. A woman compliments my skirt. I thank her as we exchange business cards. I notice she's a buyer from a showroom in Japan. She's running late so I decide not to pitch. I'll follow up later, like tomorrow. Thirty minutes later, the woman rings my cell phone. She wants to purchase the skirt. We set up an appointment and she orders it for her showroom. Transaction complete—SOH is now international!

Materials

STANDARD MATERIALS

Scissors

Marking devices

Aleene's Fabric Glue

Seam ripper

Heavy-duty straight pins

Measuring devices

Embroidery scissors

Sewing machine and sewing machine needles

Thread in matching or contrasting color

Iron and ironing board

SPECIAL MATERIALS

1 pair of jeans that fit well (or loose, as you prefer)

1. Lay jeans flat, right side out and front of jeans facing up. Mark several horizontal cutting lines on jeans legs, as shown below.

First cutting line should be at the top of the thigh, about 12 to 13 inches from top of waistband, depending on the length skirt you want.

Draw 5 horizontal lines on each leg, starting at knees. Make the space between the first and second lines 2½ inches, and the space between the remainder of the lines 4

inches. Using scissors, cut along all horizontal cutting lines, through both layers.

Trim away *inside* leg seam from each of the strips. Do NOT cut outside side seams of jeans legs; leave them intact. You will now have 10 strips—2 strips 2½ inches wide by 16 inches long, and 8 strips 4 inches wide by 16 inches long.

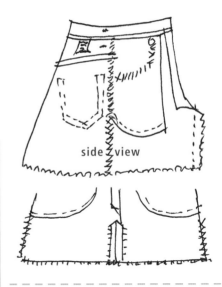

side view

2. Lay jeans top flat, right side out and front side up. Using seam ripper or embroider scissors, rip open inside leg seams and front and back crotch seams. Deconstruct extra denim layers from front and back crotch and inside leg seams (see page 37). Cut off both crotch triangles from front crotch of jeans *only*, following cutting lines as shown below, leaving ½-inch seam allowances. (Leave back crotch triangles intact.)

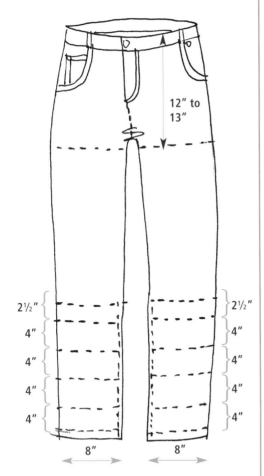

12" to 13"

2½"
4"
4"
4"
4"

2½"
4"
4"
4"
4"

8"   8"

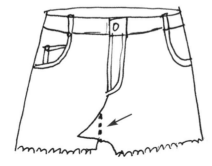

3. Turn your miniskirt inside out. Place right sides of legs together at center front, matching raw edges, and pin, as shown. (This is the center front seam of the skirt.) Stitch with ½-inch seam. Clip; with iron, press center front seam open, as shown in detail.

4. Turn skirt right side out, and lay flat with back of skirt facing up. Overlap crotch triangle from left side of jeans over crotch triangle on right side of jeans, as shown; glue. Overlap so that all layers lay flat and smooth. When glue is dry, topstitch through all layers, ⅛ inch from raw edges of crotch "triangle," as shown. Turn skirt inside out, and glue down loose edge of crotch triangle.

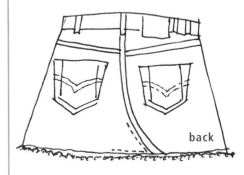

back

5. Take all 10 strips you cut in Step 1. Hand and/or machine baste each strip across one long edge, about 1 inch from edge, as shown. Pull threads from each end, gathering strips into ruffles (see page 29). You can adjust ruffles as you pin them to skirt in next step.

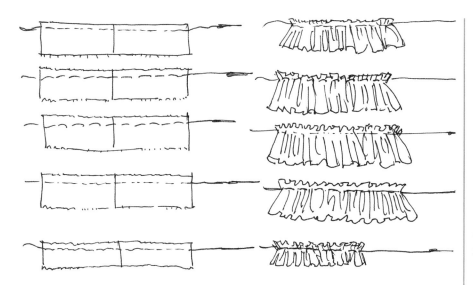

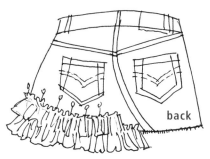

Stitch second ruffle to skirt over basting stitches (1 inch from top edge of ruffle). Remove pins.

6. Turn skirt right side out and, using 4 of the 4-inch-wide ruffles that you cut in Step 1, attach bottom ruffle to skirt.

Begin placing first ruffle at bottom of skirt front so top of ruffle is about 2 inches above hemline. Start about 14 inches from side seam, as shown, wrapping around from front to back; pin, as shown. When you get to the end of first ruffle, place another 4-inch wide ruffle so it overlaps first ruffle by about 1 inch and looks like one continuous ruffle; pin, as shown. Add third and fourth ruffle in the exact same manner. Bottom ruffle ends on back, just past the center back seam, as shown. Machine stitch bottom ruffle to skirt, over basting stitches (1 inch from top edge of ruffle). Remove pins.

7. Now position and pin second row of wide ruffles above the bottom row. Second row should overlap bottom row so that it covers stitching lines. Position and pin second row in an up-and-down fashion, as shown, so row is not in a straight line around the skirt. Be sure to overlap ruffle pieces as you add new ones, giving the effect of one long, continuous ruffle. End second ruffle on back, about 1 inch shorter than bottom ruffle, as shown in detail.

8. Use the 2 narrow ruffles for third and last row of ruffles. Beginning on opposite side of skirt front than you did for other two rows, place narrow ruffle so it overlaps stitching lines on second row of ruffles, as shown; pin. When first ruffle ends, remember to overlap it by 1/4 inch with next ruffle, so it looks like one continuous ruffle. As with second row of ruffles, third row can wrap around skirt in an up-and-down fashion, rather than in a straight line. End third row of ruffles on back, about 1 inch before second row of ruffles ends, as shown in back view; pin. Stitch third row of ruffles to skirt over basting stitches. Remove pins. Press as you like.

pants with ribbon detail

REQUIRED TIME:
25 MINUTES USING
SEWING MACHINE

45 MINUTES BY
HAND

*My denim is like
my best friends. It
endures the punches
of living and never
complains.*

— Dana Gibbs,
celebrity hairstylist
of Dana's Loft

Young at heart, these pants can be worn loose as culottes or with the bottoms gathered and the ribbon tied into bows at the calf. This pant is airy and light. To create this style, look for a pair of older wide-leg jeans that are soft with age. You need the additional fabric and softness in the denim to create the right amount of gathering at the knee.

Saqouya, a fashion heavy at her Kentucky high school, loves to be ahead of the crowd. She says: "I like to stand out—to do me. If everyone is wearing black, I'm in purple and green. When everybody was searching for dresses for homecoming, I had something else in mind. These bottoms are fly and comfortable, and I knew if I wore them I could dance, I mean dance without worry. I wore the pants with a sophisticated top, some cute wedge heels, long gold earrings, and I was the hit of the party. All my girlfriends wanted to know where I got them. And the best was, afterward I could wear them to school with a tank top. None of the girls could do that with their homecoming dresses."

Materials

STANDARD MATERIALS

Scissors

Marking devices

Aleene's Fabric Glue

Seam ripper

Heavy-duty straight pins

Measuring devices

Embroidery scissors

Sewing machine and sewing machine needles

Thread in matching or contrasting color

SPECIAL MATERIALS

1 pair wide-leg jeans with fitted waist

Large safety pin

Ribbon, 1 inch wide—20-inches plus calf measurement (for each leg)

1. Lay jeans flat, right side out, with front facing up. Mark horizontal cutting lines on legs, about 3 inches below knee level, as shown. (Use your body measurement charts to determine exact length.) Using scissors, cut along cutting line, through both layers, creating pieces A and B (which should be 8+ inches wide by 14+ inches long). Cut away inside leg seams and hems from pieces A and B, as shown below. Using seam ripper or embroidery scissors, rip apart inside leg seams *only*, (do not open seams at center front or center back.) Deconstruct excess fabric from seams (see page 37).

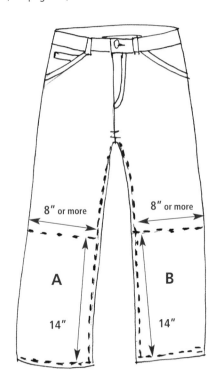

2. Take pieces A and B, cut in Step 1, and turn them so side seam runs horizontally, as shown. Draw trapezoid shape on each piece; top should be 4½ inches wide and bottom 14 inches wide, as shown below. Cut along cutting lines.

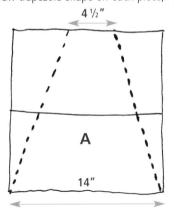

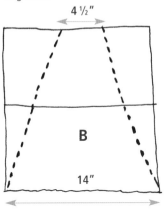

3. Fold jeans in half, right side out, on center seams. Lay them flat, on outside side seam, so inside side seam of bottom leg is facing up when you lift top leg, as shown. Fold top leg back so inside seam of bottom leg is exposed. Place trapezoid A, right side up, under opening with short end at top and wide end at bottom, overlapping raw edges ¼ inch and making sure all layers lay flat and smooth, as shown. (Leg will be wider at bottom than at top.) Using fabric glue, glue right side of A to wrong side of legs, placing glue on right of side A edges.

Turn jeans over and repeat entire process on other leg, using trapezoid B. Remember to layer something inside legs before gluing so they don't get glued together.

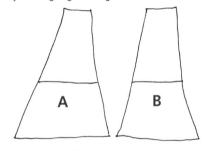

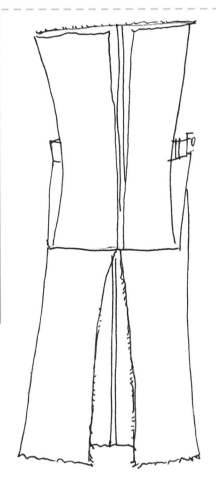

4. Once glue is dry, turn pants right side out and topstitch around insets, $\frac{1}{8}$ inch from raw edges, as shown below. Using seam ripper, open up 3 inches of outside side seams at bottom of each leg. (Side view will look like bottom illustration below).

5. With pants right side out, fold bottom edge of each leg up to inside of leg $1\frac{1}{2}$ inches; pin, from right side, as shown. On right side, stitch around bottom of each leg, 1 inch from folded edge, creating casing for drawstring as shown.

6. Pin a safety pin through one end of ribbon and insert into casing. Pull ribbon through entire casing with safety pin, as shown. Repeat on other leg.

7. Pull the drawstring from each end and tie in bows when you have the look you want—wide and loose for a relaxed look, or tight under knee for a jodhpurs/knickers look, as shown in photograph.

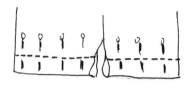

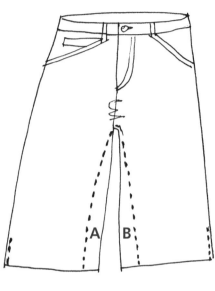

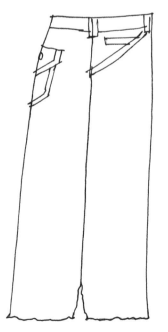

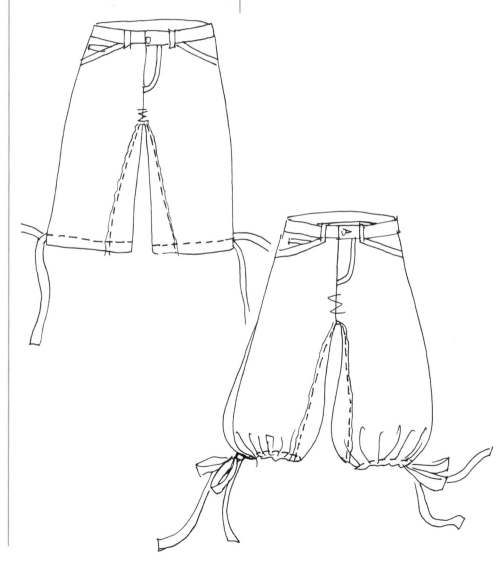

bias-trim short shorts

REQUIRED TIME:

25 MINUTES USING
SEWING MACHINE

40 MINUTES BY
HAND

Cut off vintage jeans with contrasting solid color bias trim make these the ultimate shorts—perfect for the beach on a sun-filled tropical island. Its super-short length is unapologetically sassy. You're not limited to a solid-colored bias trim, although it's the easiest to find. For a different take, look for patterned bias trims, such as plaid, argyle, or polka-dots. Wear this athletic style short with ballerina slippers and leggings: unusual combination, but the look is kittenish and refreshing.

Materials

STANDARD MATERIALS

Scissors

Marking devices

Aleene's Fabric Glue

Seam ripper

Heavy-duty straight pins

Measuring devices

Embroidery scissors

Sewing machine and sewing machine needles

Thread in matching or contrasting color

Iron and ironing board

SPECIAL MATERIALS

1 pair of tight, fitted jeans

Double-fold bias tape, 2 yards

Iron-on hemming tape

French curve

1. Lay jeans flat, right side out, with front facing up. Mark cutting lines 2 inches below crotch level on both legs, as shown below. Using scissors, cut along cutting lines, through both layers.

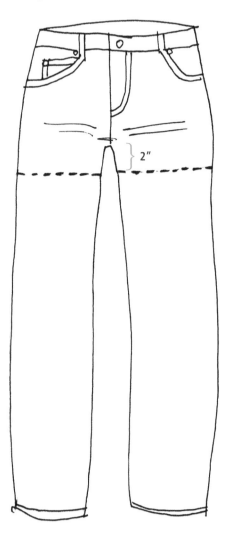

2. Lay cut-off jeans flat, right side out with front facing up. Using French curve, or any curved edge, mark rounded lines at outside bottom of each leg, as shown below. Curved line should start 3 inches up side seam, and curve down to hem, 3 inches in from side seam. Cut along cutting lines, as shown.

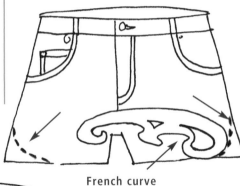

French curve

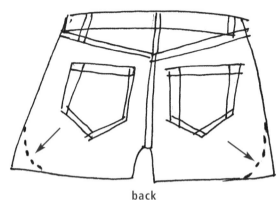

back

3. Turn jeans over so back is facing up, and repeat marking and cutting of curved lines at bottom of legs as you did on front, as shown.

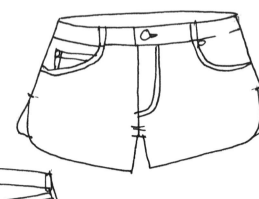

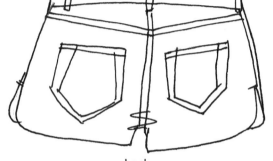

back

4. See page 36 for a shortcut for attaching bias binding around the bottom hem of shorts. Measure around bottom of leg and add 1 inch; cut out 2 lengths of bias binding and two lengths of iron-on hem tape equal to this measurement. To create bias trim, follow directions on page 36 or stitch in place.

5. The key to doing this properly is to make sure that you sandwich the shorts over the narrow part of the ironing board while you are ironing on the bias trim. Make sure that the bias trim stays flush against the edge of the hem of the shorts so that the trim does not slip.

We do not advise pinning the trim in place as the iron-on tape will leave a sticky residue on the pins, making it hard to remove them. Also, when you stitch over the pins, your stitching will not be straight. So simply take your time and go slowly while ironing on the bias trim and hold it in place by sliding your fingers over the top of the trim as you press.

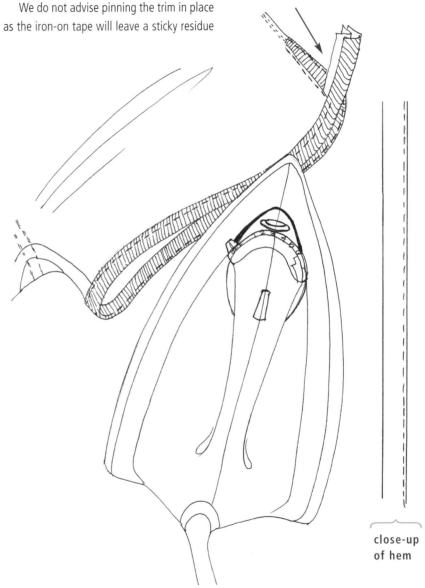

close-up of hem

2-in-1 capris

**REQUIRED TIME:
20 MINUTES USING
SEWING MACHINE**

**35 MINUTES BY
HAND**

I've always liked the idea that clothing can hold emotions and memories or connections to other people, so it wasn't a stretch to imagine a pair of jeans could be a physical repository for a living friendship.

— Ann Brashares,
author of
*The Sisterhood
of Traveling Pants*

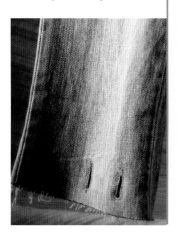

Convertible jeans, with sailor buttons at the knee, become long shorts with exposed raw edges. We pride ourselves on the multipurpose garments we design; we like clothes that can function at different levels and be suitable for various occasions, even less formal ones. For easy, weekend chic while browsing in a bookstore, reflecting in a museum, or enjoying the outdoors, wear with the bottom buttoned on. For more high style, remove the bottoms and add a d'Orsay or kitten-heeled shoe for a polished, pulled-together look.

Materials

STANDARD MATERIALS

Scissors

Marking devices

Heavy-duty straight pins

Measuring devices

Embroidery scissors

Sewing machine and sewing machine needles

Thread in matching or contrasting colors

SPECIAL MATERIALS

1 pair of fitted boot-leg or bell-bottom jeans, longer length
   than you normally wear

Embroidery needles

Embroidery floss in matching or contrasting colors

6 large buttons (1¼ inch or larger)

8 smaller buttons (½–1 inch)

NOTE: *If your machine does not make buttonholes, you'll have to find a service that will make them for you. Many dry cleaners can make buttonholes. Check local directories or local fabric stores for other sources who will make buttonholes.*

1. Lay jeans flat, right side out, with front facing up. Mark horizontal cutting lines on legs, just below the knees, as shown. Use your body measurements to determine exact length. Using scissors, cut along cutting lines, through both layers.

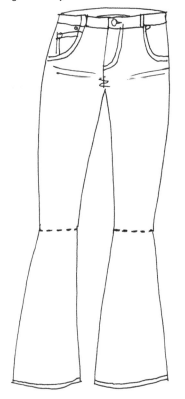

2. Lay top half of jeans flat, right side out, with front facing up, as shown. With clear pattern drafting ruler, mark 3 vertical buttonhole lines (for large buttons) at bottom of upper jeans, centering the first buttonhole, and placing the other two 1½ inches to the right and to the left of center buttonhole, as shown. Buttonholes should be ¹⁄₁₆ inch longer than your large buttons. Bottom of buttonhole lines should be half your large button width above bottom raw edge.

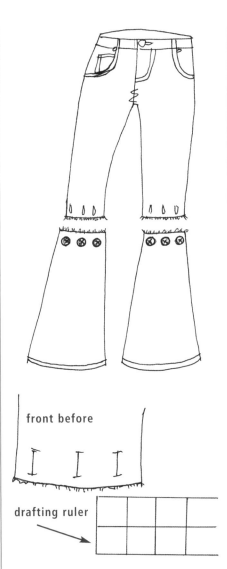

front before

drafting ruler

3. Machine-made buttonholes: Set your sewing machine to the buttonhole setting (or attach machine's buttonholer) and, using topstitching thread, make buttonholes over buttonhole lines. Trim loose threads. Using embroidery scissors, cut fabric in center of buttonhole to create opening. Some machines make keyhole buttonholes, or you can have keyholes made professionally (often by your dry cleaner.)

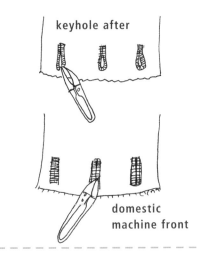

keyhole after

domestic
machine front

4. Handmade buttonholes: If the machine options are not available to you, or don't appeal to you, you can make buttonholes by hand. First cut slit in fabric along marks. Using an embroidery needle and floss, whipstitch around raw edges of each buttonhole, as shown.

Whipstitch: Insert needle at right angle, from back to front, and close to raw edge, taking tiny stitches, close together, as shown. Secure last stitch with knot and trim loose threads.

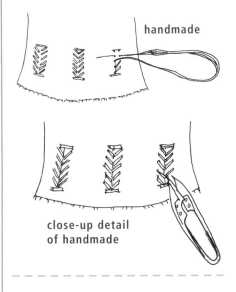

handmade

close-up detail
of handmade

5. Lay top of pants flat, right side out, with back of jeans facing up. You will use small buttons on back (large ones would run into the backs of your knees as you walk), so mark 4 vertical buttonhole lines, as shown. Evenly space 4 buttonhole lines across back, making them $\frac{1}{16}$ inch longer than your small button width, and placing them half your small button width from the bottom raw edge. As on front, make buttonholes on machine, by hand, as shown, or have a professional do it.

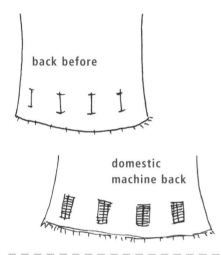

6. Lay top and bottom legs of pants flat, right side out, with front facing up. Slide bottom pant leg inside top pant leg, aligning top edge of bottom pant leg with top of buttonhole. Make sure side seams and pant legs are perfectly lined up. To mark button placement, push pencil point through buttonhole and make a mark $\frac{1}{8}$ inch from bottom of buttonhole, onto bottom pant leg. Repeat for all buttonholes. You will sew buttons at these marks.

Turn jeans over, so back sides are facing up, and repeat entire button-marking process on back of jeans.

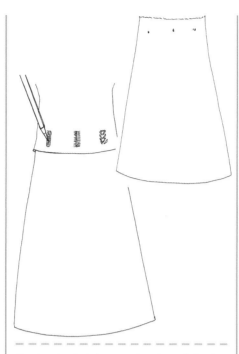

7. Hand stitch buttons in place, following button sewing tips, as shown.

There should always be at least $\frac{1}{8}$ inch of space between underside of button and fabric of garment so there is room for the extra fabric layers when buttoned up. Buttons should never be sewn flush to the garment.

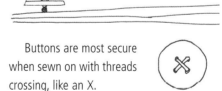

Buttons are most secure when sewn on with threads crossing, like an X.

Keep stitch placement clean by returning to same point with every stitch.

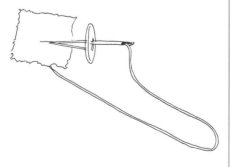

When stitch placement floats around, it looks sloppy and skews button placement, causing an ill fit.

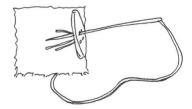

Center button over button placement mark, and, using long embroidery needle and embroidery floss, sew button in place through holes. You can start on button side of fabric or back side. Remember to stitch diagonally, to achieve the X stitching. DO NOT MAKE TIGHT STITCHES, leave a little ease. After 3 clean-through stitches, bring floss to front side of fabric, raise button up off fabric surface at least $\frac{1}{8}$ inch, then wrap floss around stitches 3 to 4 times, creating a shank for the button. Pull floss to back side; secure and trim ends. Button will be secure, but not bulky.

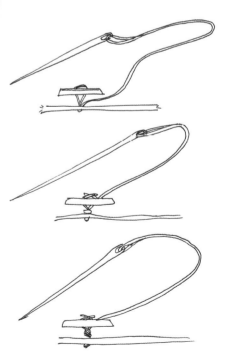

flirty a-line skirt

REQUIRED TIME:
25 MINUTES USING
SEWING MACHINE

40 MINUTES BY
HAND

*There's no denying
that denim is comfort
food for the senses of
sight and touch.*

— "Denim Does Double
Duty," *Express Textile*,
November 2005,
www.expresstextile.com

The classic A-line skirt made from a vintage pair of jeans. Our design has decorative topstitching-at the side seams and the front v-insert, but you can use any of the techniques from pages 12–15. An orbit of looks are available with this skirt. It is worn here with a red and beige sweater set, which gives it a volcanic schoolgirl appeal. Leg baring indeed, but you always have the option of tights, leggings, or legwarmers. If you're really adventurous, wear knee- or thigh-high socks to push the style envelope. This is a comfy skirt with a serious fashion range.

Materials

STANDARD MATERIALS

Scissors

Marking devices

Aleene's Fabric Glue

Seam ripper

Heavy-duty straight pins

Measuring devices

Embroidery scissors

Sewing machine and sewing machine needles

Thread in matching or contrasting color

SPECIAL MATERIALS

1 pair of very aged, washed-out jeans that fit well

Embroidery floss (your choice of color; we chose metallic)

Embroidery needle

1. Lay jeans flat, right side out, with front facing up. Mark two horizontal cutting lines on each leg, about 15–20 inches down from waist (use your body measurement charts to determine exact length), as shown. Each piece should be the same, and the entire width of leg (which is usually 8 inches or more). Using scissors, cut out pieces A and B through both front and back layers, following horizontal cutting lines, as shown. Dotted lines indicate seams that will be opened and deconstructed later.

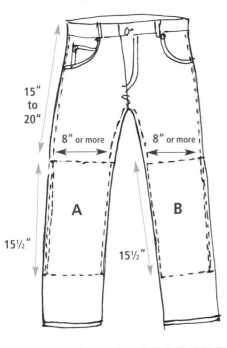

15" to 20"

8" or more   8" or more

15½"   A   B   15½"

2. Using seam ripper or embroidery scissors, rip open outside leg side seams from hem to waistband, inside leg side seams from hem to crotch point, and crotch seams from ½ inch below zipper on front, to point on back where crotch seam no longer curves, as shown. Deconstruct extra denim layers from all seams (see page 37).

Overlap left crotch triangle over right crotch triangle at center front, as shown, so all layers lay flat and smooth. Cut off end of left crotch triangle at center seam line, as shown; cut off end of right triangle ½ inch beyond center seam line. With trimmed left side on top, glue left side over right side, forming center seam, as shown. When glue is dry, topstitch ⅛ inch from raw edge.

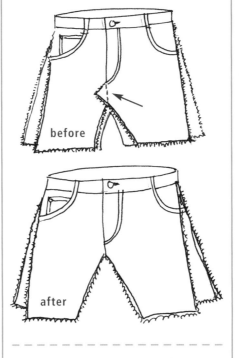

before

after

3. Turn pants over and repeat entire process on back of pants.

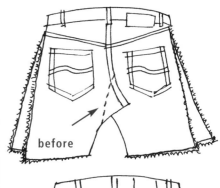

before

after

4. Take pieces A and B, cut in Step 1. Cut away side seams from each piece; you now have four identical pieces. Label 2 pieces A and 2 pieces B. Mark cutting lines on A pieces in trapezoid shape, 2 inches wide at top, 8½ inches wide at bottom, and 15½ inches tall, as shown. On B pieces, mark smaller trapezoid shapes, 3 inches wide at top, 7½ inches wide at bottom, and 8½ inches tall, as shown. Cut along cutting lines.

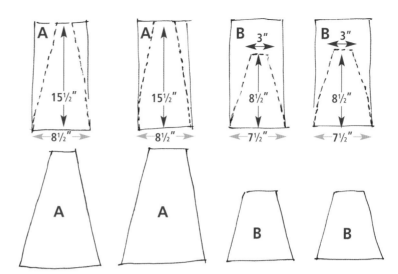

5. Lay skirt flat, right side out, and top facing up. Slide 1 piece B under center front of skirt, so all pieces lie flat and smooth, as shown. Using fabric glue, glue right side of B to wrong side of skirt front, placing glue on *wrong* side of skirt, along center front edges.

Turn skirt over so back is facing up. Glue other piece B to skirt center back in same manner as you did on the front, as shown.

Lay skirt flat on one side seam. Slide 1 piece A under open side seam, running from waistband to hemline, making sure all layers lay flat and smooth. Glue right side of piece A to wrong side of skirt side, placing glue along *wrong-side* raw edges of skirt side seams. Repeat entire process on remaining side.

6. When glue is dry, turn skirt inside out and trim excess fabric from insets, leaving ½–1 inch of fabric beyond glue line. Do not trim too close to glue line. Turn skirt right side out and topstitch along all insets through both layers, ⅛ inch from raw edges, as shown, using thread that matches jean color.

Using embroidery needle and contrasting embroidery floss, decorate skirt along insets and pocket fronts with pickstitch, as in photo. For variation, you can add any decorative stitch anywhere on skirt, as you prefer.

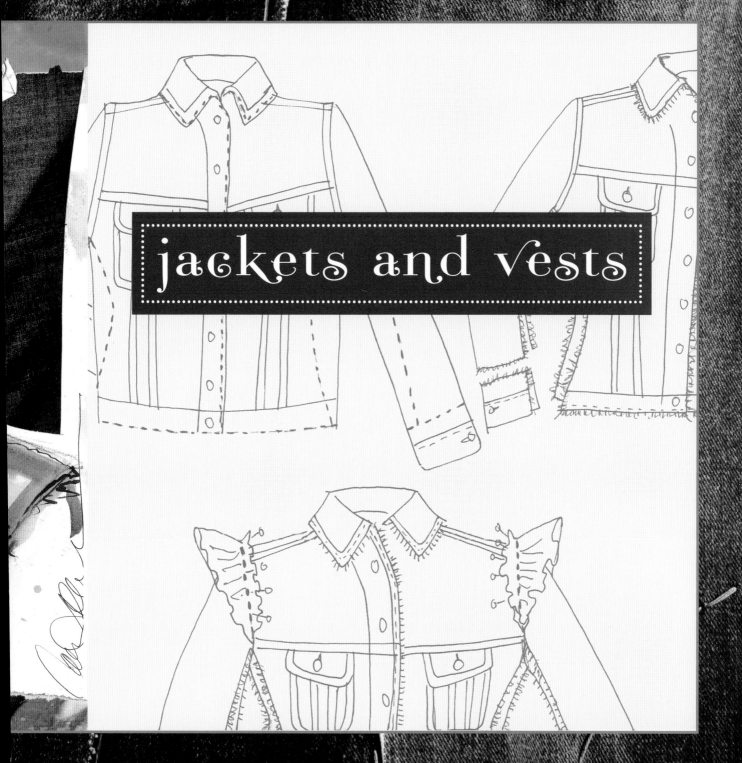

jackets and vests

long-sleeve jacket with ruffles

REQUIRED TIME:
40 MINUTES USING SEWING MACHINE

1½ HOUR BY HAND

Gone is the over-dressed formality of movie premieres and awards shows, and in its place is a relaxed attitude and the cool comfort of designer denim—so loosen that tie and unbutton that belt!

— Samantha Read, "The Denim Revolution," *Hilary Fashion*, April 17, 2006, www.hilary.com

A vintage long-sleeved denim jacket, with the edges cut and frayed for a raw deconstructed finish, is tailored to fit with tapered side seams. Use the left-over denim scraps, trimmed from the side seams, to make the sassy ruffles at the tops of the shoulders. You can wear this jacket with anything—it complements all body types. Broad shoulders or sloped shoulders, this jacket works on both and turns an ordinary outfit into a hip, runway ensemble.

Samiayah Johnson, a schoolteacher in Brooklyn, is a fashion queen. Experimental and adventurous, Samiayah seeks to find atypical, jaw-dropping garb for her wardrobe. While participating in a shopping party at Gen Art, Samiayah strode in with her ruffled denim jacket. Her breathing was heavy. We asked, "Why are you breathing so hard?" She replied, "A woman tried to purchase this jacket off my back. I told her no, but she would not leave me alone." Ten minutes before closing, a woman ran in, wild eyed, looking for the denim jacket. We didn't have any on the rack. The only one in sight was the one on Samiayah's back. She eyed Samiayah. We eyed Samiayah. Knowingly, Samiayah rolled her eyes, as she took off the jacket for the woman to purchase. Of course, we replaced Samiayah's jacket. If it happens again, she can make her own, next time.

Materials

STANDARD MATERIALS

Scissors

Marking devices

Aleene's Fabric Glue

Seam ripper

Heavy-duty straight pins

Measuring devices

Embroidery scissors

Sewing machine and sewing machine needles

Thread in matching or contrasting colors

SPECIAL MATERIALS

Denim jacket, aged and really worn, at least 1 size larger than your size

scissors, cut along cutting lines at sides and on sleeves, through both layers. Label pieces cut off from side seams A, and cut-off cuffs B. Deconstruct extra fabric layers from cuffs (see page 37). Hold A (side seam) pieces for Step 2 and B (cuff) pieces for step 5.

Unbutton jacket. Using scissors, trim seamed edges off collar, bottom of waistband, and both front plackets, as shown. Deconstruct any extra layers of fabric that remain after trimming.

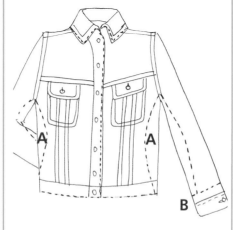

2. Take A pieces cut from side seams and, using seam ripper or embroidery scissors, rip open and deconstruct seams (see page 37). Hand or machine baste 1/2 inch from straight edge of 2 trimmed pieces. Pull basting threads from each end, gathering pieces into ruffles. Ruffle length should be half of total armhole measurement. Secure basting threads (see page 30).

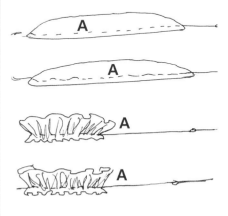

3. Turn jacket inside out. At top of sleeves, at sleeve/shoulder seam, deconstruct extra denim layers where ruffles will be pinned. Do NOT rip out seam connecting upper sleeve to jacket, just trim away some of the excess fabric layers from inside this seam (see page 37).

Turn jacket right side out. Place wrong sides of ruffles over right side of jacket at top of sleeve/shoulder seam, as shown; pin. Using sewing machine, stitch ruffles to shoulders over basting stitches, 1/2 inch from raw edge of ruffles. Remove pins.

1. Lay jacket flat, right side out with front facing up, and front of jacket fully buttoned. Mark cutting lines at side seams and on sleeve seams, as shown with dotted lines, using your body measurements to determine cutting line placements (see page 24).

Mark horizontal cutting lines at bottoms of sleeves, 1 inch above cuff, as shown. Using

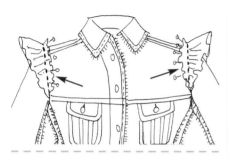

4. With jacket right side out, pin wrong side of jacket front to wrong side of jacket back at side seams and sleeves, matching underarm seams of front and back. (Note: Jacket front will be longer than jacket back, as shown in Detail.) Working on right side, stitch side seams and sleeve seams with ¼ inch seams, as shown.

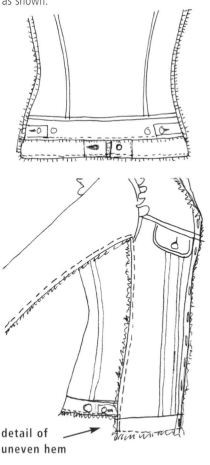

detail of uneven hem

5. Take B pieces (cuffs) and deconstruct seams at *tops* of cuffs *only*, leaving seams at bottom of cuffs intact (see page 37). With jacket right side out, slide bottom of sleeves between layers at top of cuff, so wrong sides of cuff sandwich bottom of sleeve by ½ inch. Using fabric glue, glue cuff over sleeve bottom, applying glue to top edges of cuff, on wrong side of fabric (see page 34). When glue is dry, topstitch cuff to sleeve, on right side of garment, ⅛ inch from top edge of cuff.

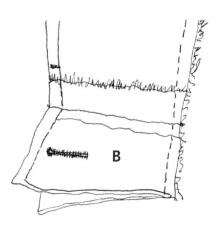

6. Topstitch around raw edges of collar, button plackets, and front and back bottom hems, ⅛ inch from raw edges, to complete the look, as shown below.

shaped sleeveless vest

REQUIRED TIME:
15 MINUTES USING
SEWING MACHINE

25 MINUTES BY
HAND

*Tattered, torn,
ripped and worn,
painted red and
white and blue.
Dressed up with
satin, downtown
with leather, cool
no matter what
weather. Denim
old and denim new,
the art of denim,
is always you.*

— www.blog.zoozoom.
com/beauty/2005/11/th
e_art_of_denim.aspx

A shapely vest made from a pale blue jacket, this is a vintage denim jacket whose sleeves have been cut off, the edges pinked and left raw. The original jacket, dating from the 1940s, came with inverted front pleats that add a whole different dimension to the top. It can be worn by women of all ages—and like the cloth it's made from, it's ageless. Flaunt the vest with a gamut of bottoms. A great layering piece, it wears well on top of T-shirts (short and long), turtlenecks, tank tops, camisoles, and traditional shirts or blouses.

Niki Hall is the cofounder of L.A.C.E.S. (Ladies About Creating Excellent Style) an image-consulting agency dedicated to helping people define their own unique sense of style through the science of interweaving, or lacing elements of one's personality with their lifestyle and fashion needs. Niki pushes the envelope with her fearless approach to wardrobe styling. She applies the same intensity when it comes to dressing herself. "I love the Sistahs DIY mentality of transforming street styles into vibrant pieces. It's unprecedented and truly inspirational."

Materials

STANDARD MATERIALS

Scissors

Marking devices

Heavy-duty straight pins

Measuring devices

Embroidery scissors

Sewing machine and sewing machine needles

Thread in matching or contrasting color

Iron and ironing board

SPECIAL MATERIALS

Lightweight denim jacket (We chose a '40s-style jacket because we liked the feminine lines and details, but any style jean jacket will work. Be sure to choose a fitted style, not one that is boxy or oversized.)

Pinking shears

1. Lay jacket flat, right side out and front facing up, with all buttons buttoned. Mark cutting lines at side seams and armholes, using your body measurements to determine cutting line placements (see page 24). Pin through all layers, just inside side seam cutting lines, as shown. Mark curved cutting lines at center front and bottom hem of jacket, as shown. Cutting line should start at second to last button on center front, and curve gracefully to side, blending up waistband into previously marked side seam cutting line, as shown here.

Using scissors, cut along all cutting lines, making sure you cut off all seams, particularly at sides of waistband.

2. Turn collar upward and carefully cut it off through the collar just above the stitched edge of the collar stand, as shown. Deconstruct extra denim layers from collar band (see page 37).

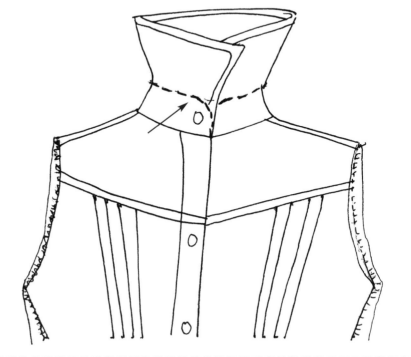

3. With jacket right side out, trim raw edges of side seams and bottom hem of jacket using pinking shears. If possible, cut through front and back of jacket simultaneously, so peaks and valleys of pinked edges match. Topstitch all pinked edges $1/8$ inch from raw edge.

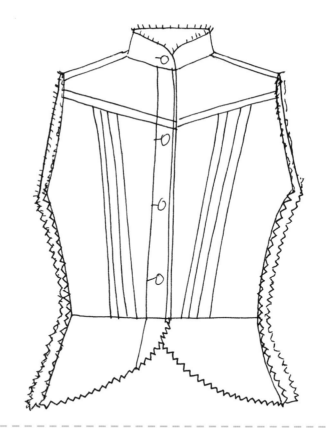

4. With jacket right side out and front facing up, match wrong side of jacket front to wrong side of jacket back at side seams, being sure to match peaks and valleys of pinked edges; pin. Stitch side seams together with $1/2$-inch seams, as shown. Using iron, press jacket, keeping all seams flat. Topstitch collar edge $1/4$ inch from raw edge.

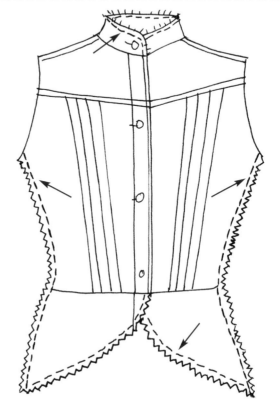

cropped jacket with sweater trim

REQUIRED TIME:
1 HOUR

Cheap or chic, there is no single piece of clothing more universal than the blue jean, an ultimate American fashion statement. America has always had a love affair with blue jeans.

— Alice Harris, author of *The Blue Jean*

S tart with a long-sleeved denim jacket and crop at the waist, leaving the edges raw. Add a bottom band cut from a vintage sweater and sewn at an angle to the lower edges of the jacket. We recommend finding a patterned vintage sweater to adapt so your jacket will be unique. Designed to be relaxed and super easy, this jacket is chameleon-like and appropriate for various occasions. We didn't taper the sides, so it is similar in shape to a traditional denim jacket, making it a very versatile piece and the perfect cover-up.

Carmia says: "Every time I wear this jacket, I feel laid back yet sharp. It's just one of those jackets I love to love."

Materials

STANDARD MATERIALS
Scissors
Marking devices
Aleene's Fabric Glue
Seam ripper
Heavy-duty straight pins
Measuring devices
Embroidery scissors
Sewing machine and sewing machine needles
Thread in matching or contrasting colors
Iron and ironing board

SPECIAL MATERIALS
Jean jacket, very fitted
Cardigan sweater, very fitted (color and pattern of your choice)

1. Lay jacket flat, right side out and front side facing up, with all buttons buttoned. Mark cutting lines at side seams and on sleeve seams, as shown, using your body measurements to determine line placement (see page 24).

Mark horizontal cutting line across bottom of jacket, just above waistband. Deconstruct extra fabric layers along any seams.

Using scissors, cut along all cutting lines, through both layers.

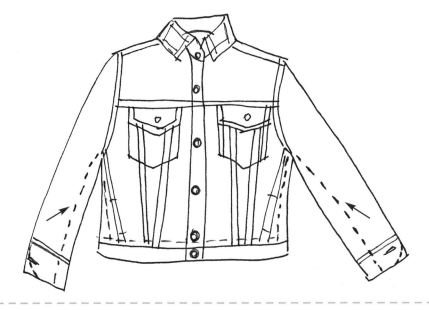

2. Button up all sweater buttons. Lay sweater flat, right side out and with front facing up. Mark horizontal cutting line at bottom of sweater, 7 inches up from bottom edge, as shown. Cut along cutting lines, through both layers, forming sweater waistband.

Zigzag stitch $1/16$ inch from raw edge of sweater waistband, making sure raw edge does not stretch out or pucker as you zigzag. Practice on unused sweater pieces first, to determine proper tension and stitch length.

3. Trim $1/4$ inch of the lower edge of jacket cuff and deconstruct extra fabric layers (see page 37). Topstitch along bottom edge of cuff.

4. Unbutton jacket and turn inside out. Lay flat, with front facing up. With right sides together, match front to back of jacket at sides and sleeves, matching armhole seams and sleeve cuffs; pin. (Note: The back of the jacket will be longer than the front at the hemline.)

Stitch $1/2$-inch side seams and sleeve seams, as shown. Remove pins. Press seams open and flat.

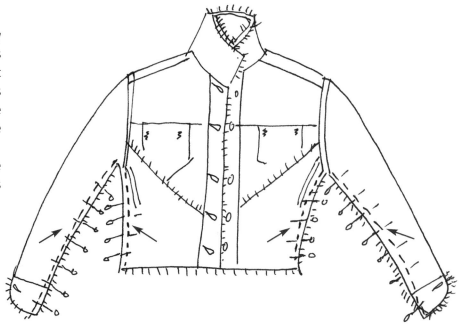

5. Trim $1/4$ inch off edges of front button plackets, and collar, deconstructing extra denim layers as necessary, (see page 37). Using fabric glue, glue together raw edges of fronts and backs of plackets and collar.

Turn jacket, still unbuttoned, right side out, and measure around entire bottom edge of jacket. Measure total length of sweater waistband, cut in Step 2. You will want these measurements to be the same.

If jacket circumference is longer than sweater waistband, take in bottom of jacket side seams until measurements match. If sweater waistband is longer than jacket measurement, make small tuck or pleat at center back of waistband until it is same length as jacket circumference.

Place sweater waistband over jacket, so right side of sweater faces right side of jacket, and raw edges match; pin, as shown. Stitch waistband to jacket with $1/2$-inch seams. Remove pins. Press waistband seam open and flat. Press jacket, keeping all seams flat.

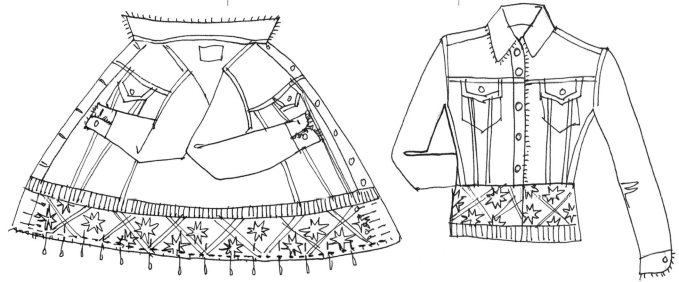

kimono jacket

REQUIRED TIME:
2 HOURS

A wardrobe without denim is like a wardrobe without water. You can only can live so long without it.

— Anonymous

nspired by traditional Asian garb, this over-the-top street couture kimono jacket is constructed from three pairs of denim pants. After completing this project, you will truly feel like a master. Deconstructed raw edges are everywhere and the exposed jean front panels on the sleeves are a fun twist. This jacket was created to perform—whether it's worn for dancing, singing, speaking, or strutting to in your world, this is not a top that sits quietly on the sidelines. Inspired by our love of kick flicks like *Crouching Tiger, Hidden Dragon*; *Hero*; *The House of Flying Daggers*; and the seductive kimonos in *Memoirs of a Geisha*.

Materials

STANDARD MATERIALS

Scissors

Marking devices

Aleene's Fabric Glue

Seam ripper

Heavy-duty straight pins

Measuring devices

Embroidery scissors

Sewing machine and sewing machine needles

Thread in matching or contrasting color

Iron and ironing board

SPECIAL MATERIALS

2 pairs of men's jeans, with wide legs (Jean size should be 33 waist/
32 length, minimum, even if you are a petite woman.)

Masking tape (for labeling fabric pieces)

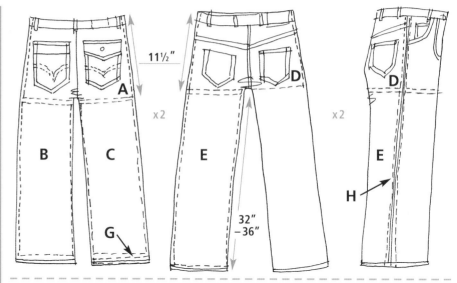

1. Lay both pairs of jeans flat, right side out, with backs facing up. Mark horizontal cutting line across entire back, 11½ inches down from top of waistband, creating pieces A and D, as shown.

Mark two vertical cutting lines 1 inch on either side of side seam, from top of waistband to bottom of leg, creating piece H, as shown with arrow.

Mark two horizontal cutting lines on each leg, near tops and bottoms of legs, creating rectangular pieces B, C, and E, as shown. Pieces B and E should be 30-plus inches long; piece C should be 28-plus inches long.

At bottom of leg with piece C, mark a horizontal line 1 inch below bottom of piece C, creating piece G, as shown. (Make sure no part of the pants hem is included in piece G.) Lay both pairs of jeans flat, right side out, with side seams facing up. Using scissors, cut completely down sides of pants, from tops of waistbands to bottoms of legs, 1 inch in on either side of centers of side seams, following cutting lines, as shown, creating 2 H pieces.

Using masking tape, label each piece with corresponding letters, as shown. Using scissors, cut along all horizontal and vertical cutting lines, through both layers. You will end up with 2 each of pieces B, C, E, and H; and 1 piece each of A, D, and G, for a total of 11 pieces.

2. Deconstruct extra denim layers on all cut pieces, as necessary (see page 37). With *right* sides together, pair up the two B, two C, and two E pieces with one another, matching all raw edges, lay flat, as shown.

3. Using your body measurements, mark cutting lines and bust dart for front bodice on *wrong* side of B and back bodice on *wrong* side of E, as shown (see page 27). Mark V-neckline on front bodice (bottom of V should be 6 inches down from neck). For (C) pieces measure out 8 to 9 inches from the straight edge. This will be the extended point on your triangle. The straight edge of your triangle should measure 13". Pin together and cut around all cutting lines, through both layers of denim.

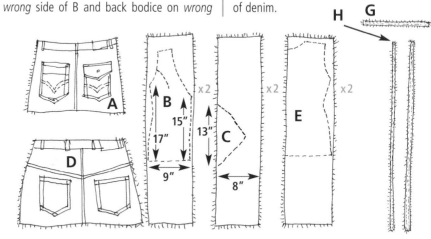

4. Topstitch close to all raw edges of 2 H pieces (belt ties) and 1 G piece (back belt), set aside. On front bodice pieces (B), stitch darts together, as shown. (See page 42, Step 7.)

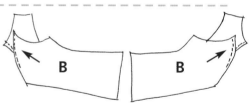

5. Match two back bodice pieces (E) at center backs, right sides together; pin, then stitch $1/2$-inch seam. Turn inside out; using iron, press center back seam open and flat. To make tucks for shaping on back bodice, turn back bodice right side faceup. Halfway between center back and each side seam, pinch $1/2$ to 1 inch of fabric, and fold it over toward each side, forming tucks. Pin tucks in place, placing pins horizontally, then topstitch close to each folded edge of tuck, from armhole level to 2 inches below waist, as shown below.

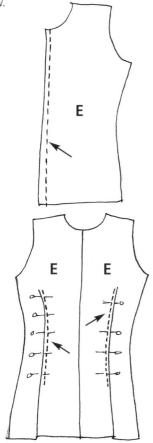

6. Lay front bodice pieces (B) and front extension pieces (C) flat, with right side face up. Overlap pieces at center front seams by **1 inch** and glue, using fabric glue (see page

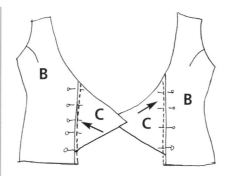

34), or pin. When glue is dry, stitch through both layers, about $1/4$ inch from raw edge, as shown above.

- -

7. Place front bodice and back bodice with right sides together, matching front to back at shoulder seams and side seams; pin as shown. Stitch together at shoulders and at sides with $1/2$-inch seams.

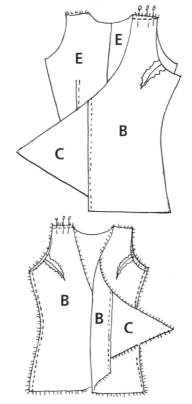

8. Lay bodice flat, right side out with back facing up, as shown at right above. Glue back

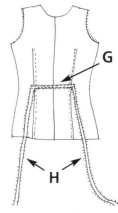

belt (G) across center back, at waist level; then overlap 1 inch at one end of each belt tie (H) over both ends of back belt (G) and glue. When glue is dry, stitch back belt and ends of belt ties to back, close to all raw edges.

- -

9. To make jacket sleeves, use pieces A and D. Place waistband edges of A and D over each shoulder seam, with wrong side of sleeves (A and D) facing right side of bodice, as shown below.

On front bodice, glue (or pin) entire length of "waistband" to bodice front; on back, glue (or pin) "waistband" to bodice from shoulder seam, down 5 to 6 inches.

When glue is dry, stitch sleeves to bodice $1/8$ inch in from outside edge of waistband, then again 1 inch in from outside edge, as shown below.

cinched-waist jacket

REQUIRED TIME:
45 MINUTES

Made using a standard long-sleeved jacket with the cuffs removed, the sleeves are left raw and slits added. A clever cinched-in waist treatment is created using the cuffs to create a tapered effect at the waistline. Add appliqués of mixed fabric at the shoulder, sleeve, or elbow if desired. Shown here with green Chinese brocade on the left shoulder, you can use the fabric of your choice. We recommend using a contrasting color so the detail will pop. So versatile it can be worn with any bottom—they all work.

N'Dea Davenport, a brilliant solo artist and the lead vocalist for the band Brand New Heavies is known for her keen, authentic fashion sense. She is eclectic and funky and has been spotted rocking a similar jacket on more than one occasion. "My SOH jacket is like a dope T-shirt—you can wear it with anything! What sets it off for me is the Chinese brocade on the shoulder. I can dress it up with a pair of pumps, an elegant pant, or wear it with some old-school Adidas. At home in NYC or touring across the globe, I make sure to always include my favorite jacket from SOH."

Materials

STANDARD MATERIALS

Scissors

Marking devices, two colors

Aleene's Fabric Glue

Seam ripper

Heavy-duty straight pins

Measuring devices

Embroidery scissors

Sewing machine and sewing machine needles

Thread in matching or contrasting colors

Iron and ironing board

SPECIAL MATERIALS

1 dark denim jacket, 1 size larger than a perfect fit

¼ yard of silk jacquard or fabric of your choice

Tracing paper

2. Deconstruct all extra denim layers from cuffs (see page 37).

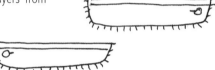

3. To make patterns for shoulder appliqués, lay jacket right side up, with bodices and sleeves completely flat, as shown. Place tracing paper over one shoulder, so tracing paper covers front and back yoke. Mark lines for appliqué patterns, following armhole, shoulder and side seam of jacket; the other edges can be any shape desired.

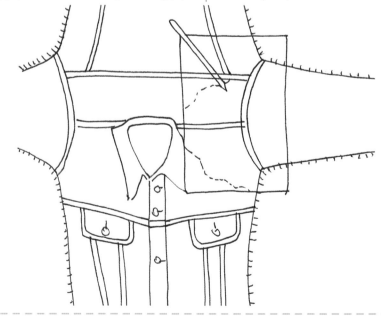

1. Lay jacket flat, right side out, with front facing up, and front of jacket fully buttoned. Mark cutting lines at side seams and on sleeve seams, as shown, using your body measurements to determine cutting line placement (see page 24).

Mark horizontal cutting lines at bottom of sleeves, 1 inch above cuff. Using scissors, cut along cutting lines at sides and on sleeves, through both layers. Set cuffs to the side.

4. Cut out tracing paper pattern. Place patterns on fabric, and mark outlines. Cut out shoulder appliqués, using scissors.

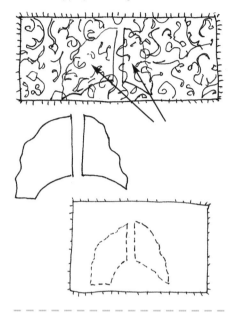

5. With jacket bodice and sleeves laying right side out and completely flat, place appliqués over shoulder, on each side of shoulder seam, as shown; glue in place with fabric glue (see page 34). When glue is dry, topstitch appliqués to shoulder, $\frac{1}{8}$ inch from raw edges of fabric.

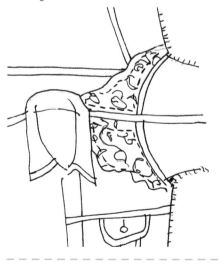

6. Turn jacket inside out. With *right* sides together, pin front of jacket to back, matching sleeves, armholes, and side seams. Stitch with $\frac{1}{2}$-inch seams, as shown, leaving a 2-inch opening for slit at bottom of sleeve.

7. Turn jacket right side out. Using cuffs cut from jacket in Step 1, place cuffs on front bodice of jacket at waistline (about $4\frac{1}{2}$ inches from bottom edge of jacket), starting on front and wrapping around side, as shown; glue in place. When glue is dry, topstitch around all raw edges of "cuff," as shown. Using iron, press jacket, keeping all seams flat.

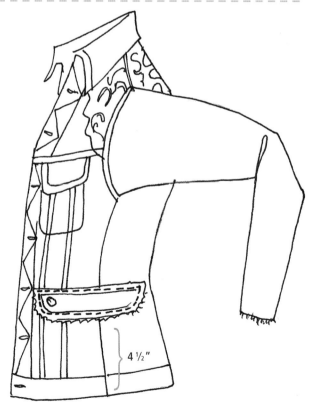

4 1/2"

jacket with sweatshirt sleeves and collar

REQUIRED TIME:

1 HOUR

Why not combine two of the most comfortable items on the planet—the sweatshirt and the jean? This piece is crafted from a vintage denim jacket, with sleeves and collar removed and replaced with sleeves and a ruffled collar made from a sweatshirt. The ruffled collar has a gentle Victorian feeling and pops up to outline your face. The fitted bodice defines your waist for a casual yet regal style. As you know, you're not limited to our suggestions. Go for it, peeps! If you're feeling daring, use a printed sweatshirt. The sky is the limit. Explore!

Mary Geghlar, fashion director of Gen Art, says: "A charming take on a simple denim jacket! The ruffles and soft sleeves are not only feminine and full of personality, but the sweatshirt material is a lot cozier than stiff denim."

Materials

STANDARD MATERIALS

Scissors

Marking devices

Aleene's Fabric Glue

Seam ripper

Heavy-duty straight pins

Measuring devices

Embroidery scissors

Sewing machine and sewing machine needles

Thread in matching or contrasting colors

Iron and ironing board

SPECIAL MATERIALS

1 jean jacket, 1 size larger than perfect fit

1 sweatshirt, fitted or 1 size large for more dramatic sleeves

1. Lay jacket flat, right side out, with front facing up and front of jacket fully buttoned. Mark cutting lines at side seams and on sleeve seams, as shown, using your body measurements to determine cutting line placements (see page 24). Using scissors, cut along cutting lines.

Turn collar up and carefully cut it off by cutting through the collar just above the stitched edge of the collar stand, as shown. Deconstruct extra denim layers from collar stand and side and armhole seams, as necessary (see page 37).

2. Lay sweatshirt flat, right side out, with front facing up. Cut off both sleeves (B), just inside seam lines, as shown. Mark two horizontal lines across front, 2 to 2½ inches apart, as shown (A). Cut along cutting lines, through front layer of sweatshirt only. This piece will be the ruffled collar.

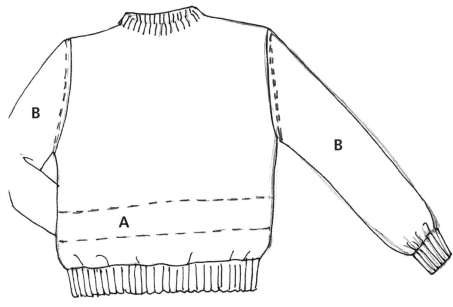

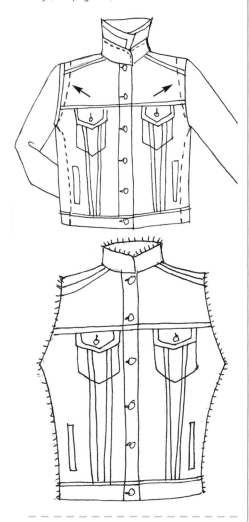

3. Lay collar (A) flat; mark rounded corners at top edges, as shown below, and cut following lines. Zigzag stitch around raw edges of collar at sides and top, to prevent fraying.

Hand or machine baste 1 inch from long bottom edge of collar, as shown (see page 30). Pull basting threads from both ends of collar in a drawstring motion, gathering until collar is same length as collar stand; spread gathers evenly.

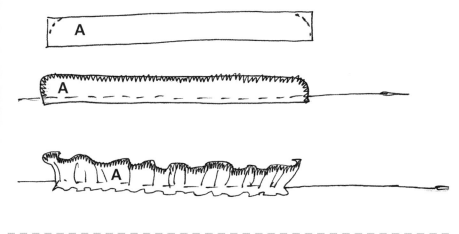

4. Making sure collar stand has been deconstructed, insert gathered edge of collar (A) between inside and outside layers of collar stand, as shown. Right side of gathered collar should face out. Glue (see page 34) or pin in place. When glue dries, topstitch $\frac{1}{8}$ inch from raw edge of collar stand, as shown below.

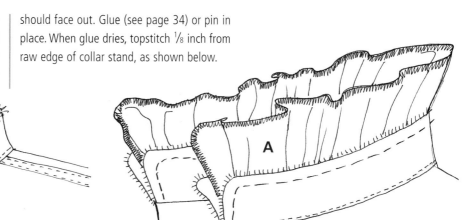

5. Turn jacket inside out; turn sleeves inside out. With right sides together, pin jacket at side seams, matching armholes and hems; stitch with $\frac{1}{2}$-inch seams and remove pins.

With right sides facing, pin sleeves into armholes, matching underarm seams and center of sleeves to shoulder seam of jacket; pin, then stitch with $\frac{1}{2}$-inch seams. Remove pins; using iron, press seams flat. Turn right side out.

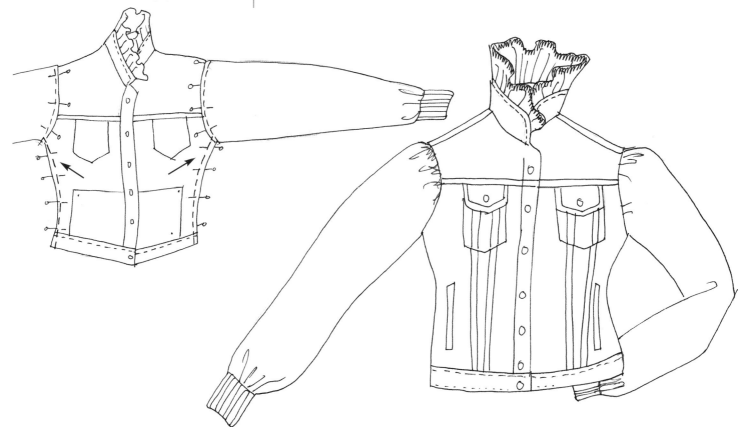

accessories

deconstructed scarf

*Denim has truly
attained the status
of a universal fabric,
is a continuing
classic, and notwith-
standing, at times,
maddening idiosyn-
crasies, can be fun
to sew!*

— Cherly Ellex, Bella
Online's sewing editor,
"Indomitable Denim,"
www.bellaonline.com

An easy-to-make deconstructed denim scarf with pockets. It can be embellished with any technique from pages 12–15. Flowing and unrestricted, it's
designed to move with the wind despite its innate durability. Add some flam-
boyance and funk to a conservative look just by throwing it on. Remember when
making this style, to wash, wash, and wash your denim until it feels soft to your hand.

*Deanna Haines, founder of Zen Home cleaning, stands by her denim scarf. She claims it's
her "attract a new client" accessory. We love it! One day while visiting a client, Deanna wore
the deconstructed scarf. The client, already satisfied with Zen Home services, started to
admire her wardrobe. Specifically, the scarf held her attention. Deanna imitates her cus-
tomer's voice: "Where did you get this scarf? It's glorious. There's something very organic
about this thing. Maybe it's the raw edges. I would like to own one for myself." Tickled,
Deanna passed along our card. She playfully told her, "Call them, they'll teach you how to
make it."*

Materials

STANDARD MATERIALS

Scissors

Marking devices

Aleene's Fabric Glue

Heavy-duty straight pins

Measuring devices

Sewing machine and sewing machine needles

Thread in matching or contrasting colors

Iron and ironing board

SPECIAL MATERIALS

1 pair of very worn jeans, any size

Fabric softener

1. Scarf is made from 10 pieces, cut from the front and back of jeans.

Using seam ripper and embroidery scissors, cut jeans front away from jeans back at side seams and inseams (inner legs); cut completely through waistband at side seams, using fabric scissors.

Lay jeans front flat, right side facing up. Mark horizontal and vertical cutting lines, as shown, creating pieces 1, 2, 3, and 4. Vertical

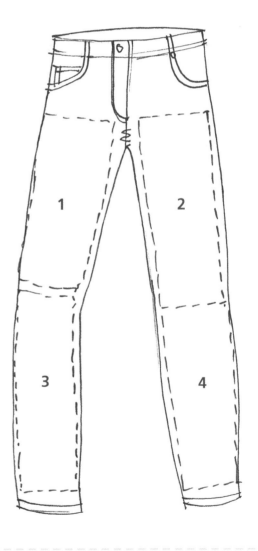

cutting lines should be 1 inch from original seam lines. Make 4 pieces 24 inches long. Using scissors, cut out all 4 pieces along cutting lines.

----

2. Lay jeans back flat, right side up. Mark horizontal and vertical cutting lines to create pieces 5, 6, 7, 8, 9, and 10, as shown below. (5 = 3 inches by 22 inches; 6 = 4$\frac{1}{2}$ inches by 20 inches; 7 = 2$\frac{1}{2}$ inches by 19$\frac{1}{2}$ inches; 8,

9, and 10 = 1 inch by 23 inches.) Cut out pieces 5–10 along cutting lines.

----

3. With right sides facing up, lay pieces 1, 2, and 3 in a vertical row, overlapping short edges by $\frac{1}{2}$ inch, as shown. Using fabric glue (see page 34), glue overlapped short edges, (1 over 2; 2 over 3.) When glue is dry, topstitch through both layers, close to raw edges, as shown in blue, creating base scarf.

Following illustration, position and glue top and bottom edges of piece 4 over base scarf; when glue is dry, topstitch through all layers, close to raw edges of piece 4. Position, glue, and topstitch piece 5, and then 6, to base scarf in same manner as piece 4. Position, glue, and then stitch all 4 raw edges of piece 9 over base scarf. Position, glue, and stitch top edges *only* of pieces 7, 8, and 10 to base scarf, through all layers.

Wash scarf with fabric softener to soften; then press with iron if desired.

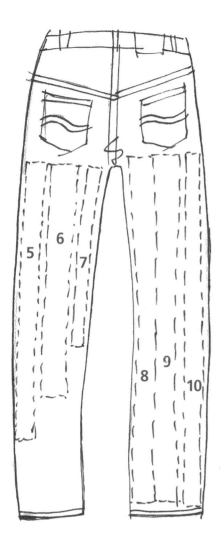

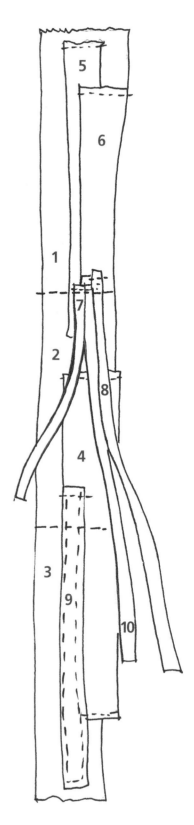

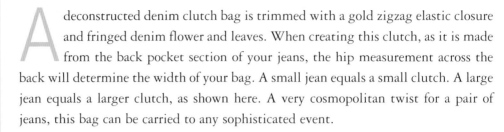

large clutch bag

**REQUIRED TIME:
45 MINUTES TO
1 HOUR**

*I not only wear
denim but also sleep
on denim. My duvet
looks good in blue.*

— Anonymous

A deconstructed denim clutch bag is trimmed with a gold zigzag elastic closure and fringed denim flower and leaves. When creating this clutch, as it is made from the back pocket section of your jeans, the hip measurement across the back will determine the width of your bag. A small jean equals a small clutch. A large jean equals a larger clutch, as shown here. A very cosmopolitan twist for a pair of jeans, this bag can be carried to any sophisticated event.

Kendall Farr, author of the Pocket Stylist *(Gotham Books, 2004) loves the denim clutch bag. She states, "A brilliant idea and every crafty girl's dream bag. Easy to make and a classic, elegant bag shape in denim that goes anywhere. An ideal bag to personalize with trim, beads, or to embroider with your monogram. Love it."*

Materials

STANDARD MATERIALS

Scissors

Marking devices

Aleene's Fabric Glue

Heavy-duty straight pins

Measuring devices

Sewing machine and sewing machine needles

Thread in matching or contrasting colors

Iron and ironing board

SPECIAL MATERIALS

1 pair of dark jeans with great back pocket designs and in fairly
    good shape (The size of the clutch you want determines what
    size jeans you'll work with.)

Gold or metallic elastic, ¼ inch wide (½ yard)

Hand-sewing needle

Illustration board

Box cutter or mat knife

NOTE: *Before you begin, decide what size clutch you'd like. If you prefer it
    small and dainty, use size 4–6 jeans; for a medium clutch, use size 8–10
    jeans; for a dramatic, large clutch (as shown here), use size 12 jeans*

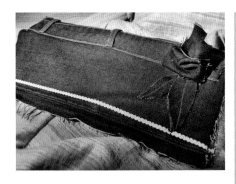

1. Lay jeans flat, right side out, with back facing up. Mark horizontal cutting line across entire back of jeans, 10 inches down from waistband, and 2 vertical cutting lines along each side seam from waistband to this horizontal line, as shown for piece A.

On both legs, mark cutting lines for pieces B and C, beginning above knee level, 7 inches wide and 18 inches long, as shown. Mark cutting line on outside leg seam of piece C, but do NOT mark cutting line along outside leg seam of piece B—this outside leg seam (on B) should remain intact.

On one leg, mark cutting lines for piece D (2½ inches wide by 15 inches long) and, square piece E, 4½ by 4½ inches, as shown.

Using scissors, cut along all cutting lines, through both layers for pieces B, C, and E, and through pants back only for pieces A and D. REMEMBER: Do NOT cut outside leg seam of piece B.

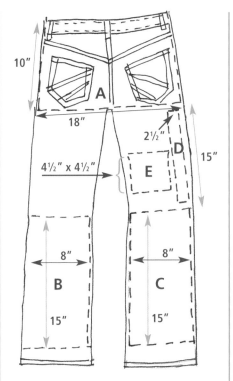

2. Deconstruct extra fabric layers from pieces A, C, and the cut edge of B (see page 37), if necessary.

With wrong sides together, match the 2 C pieces; pin. Fold the B piece in half; pin. Using sewing machine, stitch B together with ½-inch seams, along all 3 raw edges, as shown. Stitch C pieces together with ½-inch seam along 3 sides, leaving 1 short side free, as shown. Press pieces A–E.

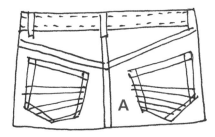

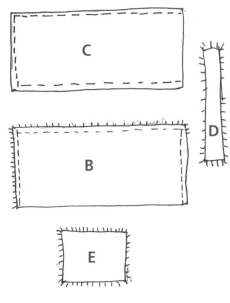

3. Using box cutter, cut a rectangle from the illustration board, 14 inches long by 7 inches high. Slide cut illustration board into open end of piece C, keeping all seams on outside; stitch together open end of piece C through both layers, with ½-inch seam, as shown below, enclosing illustration board. This will be the front.

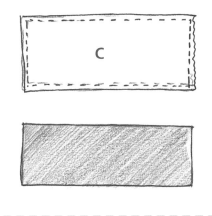

4. Lay piece A (purse back) flat, right side facing up. Place piece B (flap), underneath purse back A, so A overlaps B by 2½ inches at waistband, as shown. Using fabric glue (see page 34), glue A to B where it overlaps. When glue dries, stitch A and B together, through all layers, about ¼ inch from top edge of waistband.

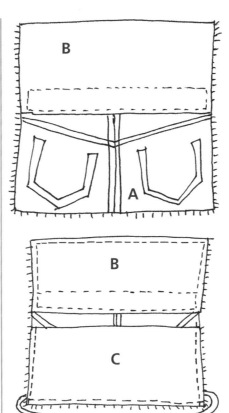

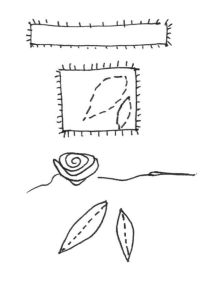

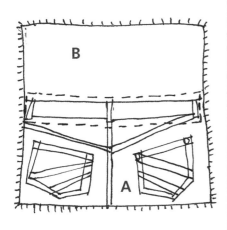

5. Cut a length of elastic, 3 inches shorter than long edge of C. Using zigzag stitch, stitch elastic to one long edge of purse front C, stretching elastic so it goes across front from edge to edge 1 inch up from bottom.

Lay joined back (A) and flap (B), flat, with *wrong* side of A facing up. Place purse front C, over A, as shown, and elastic edge of C at bottom. Glue (or pin) along 3 outside edges; when glue is dry, topstitch through both layers, ¼ inch from all outside raw edges, as shown. (Note that C does not completely cover A; you need some extra space at the top so B folds over smoothly.)

6. Make a fabric rose from piece D: pinch and roll 1 long edge of D into a tight roll, as shown (this is bottom of rose); other long edge will flutter out to create rose petals. Using handsewing needle and thread, stitch bottom of rose, securing the tight roll.

Stack the 2 E pieces together and mark leaf shapes on top piece; cut out leaf shapes through both layers. Glue leaf layers together, to form 2 leaves. When glue is dry, stitch down center of each leaf, as shown.

7. Fold flap B over purse front. Using hand-sewing needle and thread, sew leaves just below third belt loop on flap, as shown below. Next, handsew rose over belt loop, at top of leaves.

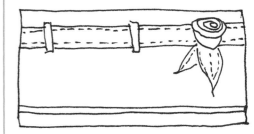

fanny pack

REQUIRED TIME:
35 MINUTES

Amazingly wonder-
ful androgynous
material. Couples
can share pants
and make love.
Who could ask
for more?

— Anonymous

A deconstructed denim waistband is turned into a funkafied fanny pack made with a jeans pocket turned inside out. Add two colored zippers, and finish using any technique you choose from pages 12–15. For extra fun, dangle a few charms from the zipper. Who says a fanny pack is only for your grandmother? This version can hold your bare essentials: cell phone, lip gloss, and keys, and still look outstanding on top of skirts and pants—making it a truly practical style accessory.

Materials

STANDARD MATERIALS

Scissors

Marking devices

Aleene's Fabric Glue

Seam ripper

Heavy-duty straight pins

Measuring devices

Sewing machine sewing machine needles

Thread in matching or contrasting color

Iron and ironing board

SPECIAL MATERIALS

1 pair of really worn jeans that are 1 size larger than your size,
   so fanny pack will hang on your hip line

10-inch zipper (any kind; any color)

12-inch zipper (any kind; any color)

2 to 3 charms on clip key ring chains

Cotton thread (bright colors)

1. Lay jeans flat, right side out, with front facing up. Mark cutting lines on front around waistband just below belt loop level; then, just after fly, curve a line down the front, around pocket level to side seam, as shown. Turn jeans over. Mark cutting lines around top of jeans back: continuing from front, go around waistband just below belt loop level; then, just after center back seam, curve a line down the back, around a back pocket, to side seam, as shown. Adjust curved lines on front and back so they meet at side seams.

Using scissors, carefully cut along cutting lines on front and back (A), through 1 layer *only*, leaving waistband intact. Be sure to cut just below belt loops; do not cut them off. Be careful to cut through just one layer at a time; do not cut the front and back simultaneously.

Lay jeans flat, with back facing up. On 1 leg, mark cutting lines for piece B, 8 inches wide by 17½ inches long, as shown. Cut along cutting lines, through both layers, leaving inside leg seam intact. (Do NOT cut open inside leg seam.)

At bottom of leg, cut small piece C, ½ inch by 3½ inches through 1 layer.

Deconstruct seams as necessary (see page 37).

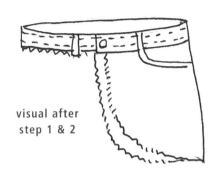

visual after step 1 & 2

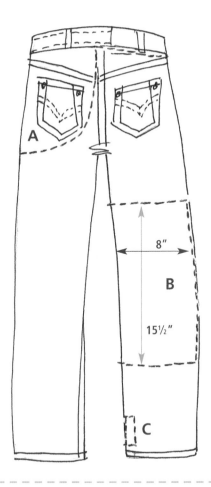

2. Open piece B; with iron, press seam flat. Lay B, *wrong* side up (with seam running horizontally) as shown below.

Lay piece A, right side facing up, on top of B, so that wrong sides of pieces A and B are together, as shown. (This will allow the fanny pack to be reversible.)

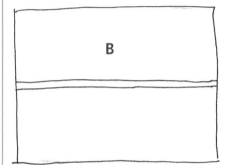

Trace around perimeter of A (*not* including waistband) onto B, as shown, to create piece D. (Top of piece D is just below waistband on piece A.) Cut out piece D along cutting lines, as shown at right above.

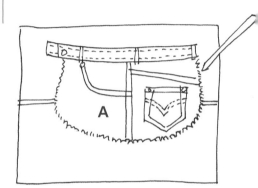

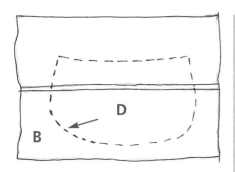

3. Lay piece D flat, right side facing up. Mark 8-inch-long line at lower left, as shown below. Using scissors, cut a slit along this line.

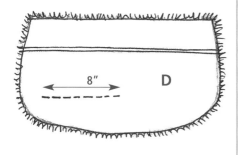

4. Place 10-inch zipper so it is centered over 8-inch slit. Using fabric glue, glue edges of zipper tape to D (see page 34). When glue is dry, stitch zipper, $1/8$–$1/4$ inch from outside edges of zipper tape. If using machine, switch to zipper foot. This is a functioning zipper, so be sure to stitch across ends, reinforcing ends and corners of zipper.

Fold piece C (cut in Step 1) into thirds, so it is about the same size as a belt loop. Glue top and bottom edges of loop C to D; when glue dries, stitch C to D, $1/8$ inch from top (at top left hand corner as shown at right above) and bottom edges of loop C.

Place 12-inch zipper off center, and above 10-inch zipper. Glue edges of zipper to D. When glue dries, stitch zipper to D, $1/8$ inch from edges of zipper tape. This is a nonworking, decorative zipper.

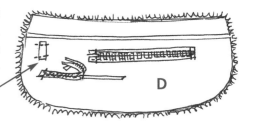

5. Lay A flat, with wrong side facing up (i.e., pockets facing down.) Lay D on top of A, with wrong side facing down matching curved edges; pin around curved edges.

Stitch D to A, $1/4$ inch from curved edge, as shown; remove pins. Stitch across top of D, through both layers, $1/4$ inch below waistband of A, as shown.

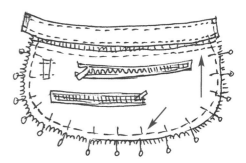

6. Press. Attach keys, charms, costume jewelry, bangles, etc. to belt loops and loop C, as shown, for a touch of fun.

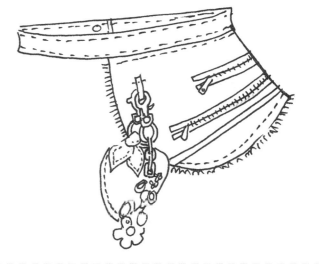

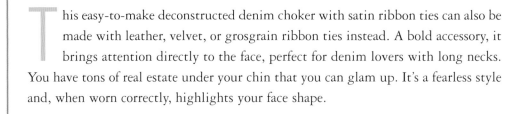

choker with ribbon trim

This easy-to-make deconstructed denim choker with satin ribbon ties can also be made with leather, velvet, or grosgrain ribbon ties instead. A bold accessory, it brings attention directly to the face, perfect for denim lovers with long necks. You have tons of real estate under your chin that you can glam up. It's a fearless style and, when worn correctly, highlights your face shape.

Materials

STANDARD MATERIALS

Scissors

Marking devices

Aleene's Fabric Glue

Seam ripper

Heavy-duty straight pins

Measuring devices

Sewing machine and sewing machine needles

Thread in matching or contrasting color

Iron and ironing board

SPECIAL MATERIALS

1 scrap, minimum 6 inches by 20 inches, from a pair of really
worn, "soft" jeans

Velcro®, 1-inch wide, 3½ inches long (Velcro has two surfaces,
the hook and the loop, which adhere to one another)

Decorative ribbons, ½-inch or 1½-inch wide (your choice), in 36-
to 40-inch lengths (the wider width will be more dramatic)

Curved ruler or French curve

1. Lay fabric flat, right side out. Mark cutting lines for neck choker (A), as shown. Choker length should equal your neck measurement (from your body measurement chart; see page 20), plus 2 inches (ease for Velcro closure). Choker width should be 4½ inches at each end, curving out to 6 inches at center, as shown below.

Also mark 2 small pieces (B), 1 inch by 2½ inches. Using scissors, cut out A and B pieces, through 1 layer only.

2. Topstitch around all sides of choker A, ¼ inch from all raw edges. Or, for a more crafty look, hand pickstitch ¼ inch from all raw edges. For a little extra flair, cut choker out with pinking shears, as shown.

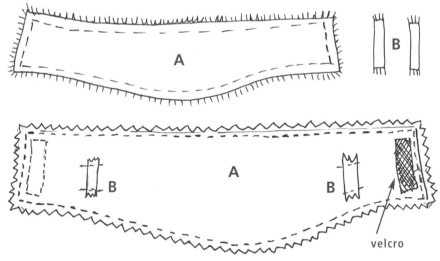

velcro

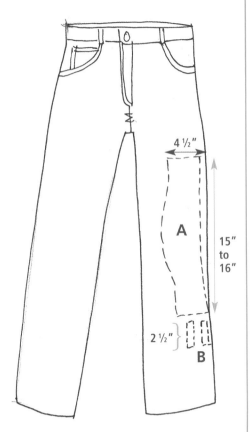

4½"

A

15" to 16"

2½"}

B

3. Lay choker right side up. Place 2 small B pieces onto *right* side of choker, 3 inches in from ends and centered between topstitching; stitch each B piece to choker at top and bottom edges, as shown.

Cut Velcro into a 3½-inch length. Place the *hook* piece of Velcro on *wrong* side of choker, ½ inch in from edge and centered between topstitching, as shown. Glue with fabric glue; when glue is dry, stitch around edges to secure (see page 34). Place the *loop* piece of Velcro at the opposite end of choker on *right* side of choker, ¼ inch from end, and centered between topstitching. Glue and stitch in same manner. (Note: The hook side is attached to wrong side of choker and the loop side is attached to right side of choker.)

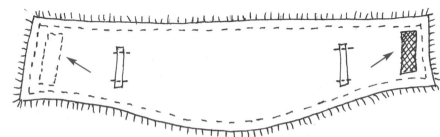

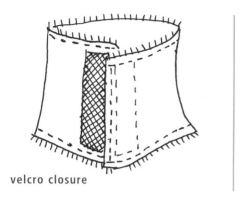

velcro closure

4. Put choker around your neck, and close. Thread ribbon of your choice through B loops, as shown. Note the different looks created by using different ribbon widths.

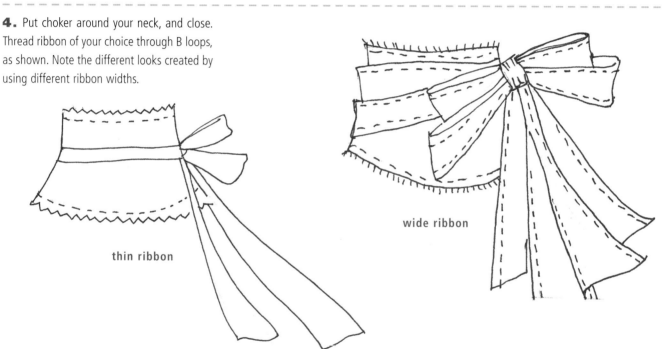

thin ribbon

wide ribbon

obi-style wrap belt

REQUIRED TIME:
45 MINUTES USING
SEWING MACHINE

1½ HOURS BY
HAND

*You know what
comes between me
and my Calvins?
Nothing.*

— Brooke Shields,
   Calvin Klein ad, 1980

Add another dimension to any outfit with this deconstructed denim obi-style wrap belt. It's a clever way to define the waist. Wrap it up and pull it in, the obi belt is an awesome waist cincher that works over a multitude of tops or dresses. It's a great layering piece. Change the ribbon for a variety of looks. We like to call it a transformer obi: pull it out and it changes your entire look.

Materials

STANDARD MATERIALS

Scissors

Marking devices

Aleene's Fabric Glue

Heavy-duty straight pins

Measuring devices

Sewing machine and sewing machine needles

Thread in matching or contrasting colors

Iron and ironing board

SPECIAL MATERIALS

1 pair of jeans, any size, 32-inch+ length, well worn, so denim
   is soft and pliable

Scrap leather (from shoe repair stores, fabric stores, or, recycle
   old leather clothes, gloves, belts or purses, as long as the
   leather is very soft and pliable)

Ribbon, or 2 ribbons, each 1-inch wide and at least
   36 inches long

1. Lay jeans flat, right side out, with front facing up. Mark cutting lines for main belt (piece 1), belt appliqués (pieces 2, 3, 4, and 5) and belt loops (pieces 6 and 7), as shown. Length of main belt (1) should be 2 inches *less* than your waist measurement; width should be 7 inches. Note: the two long edge measurements are slightly different.

Appliqué pieces (2, 3, 4, and 5) can be varying lengths, widths, and shapes, as shown. Belt loop pieces (6 and 7) should be 1 inch wide and 6 inches long.

Using scissors, cut out all 7 pieces along cutting lines, through 1 layer only.

2. Lay main belt (1) flat, right side up. Arrange denim appliqué pieces 2–5 on belt, to your taste; glue with fabric glue (see page 34). When glue is dry, topstitch around raw edges, using colorful, contrasting threads, as shown.

For belt loops, place loops 6 and 7 vertically at each end of belt, 1/4 inch from edges, as shown. Stitch (do NOT glue) loops to belt 1/8 inch from top and bottom edges. Stitch 2 more rows across belt loops, about 1 1/2 to 1 3/4 inches apart, creating 3 separate openings in each belt loop, as shown below. (You will lace ribbons through these loops to tie belt closed.)

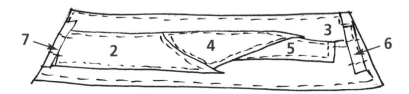

3. Using scissors, cut appliqué pieces (A and B) from leather scraps or recycled clothes or accessories, as shown. A and B can be any dimension and shape you desire. Glue leather appliqués A and B to right side of belt, over denim appliqués, as shown. When glue is dry, topstitch around appliqués, using colorful, contrasting thread. If you like, you can add random, colorful stitching around the belt, also.

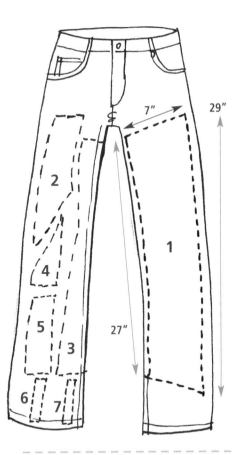

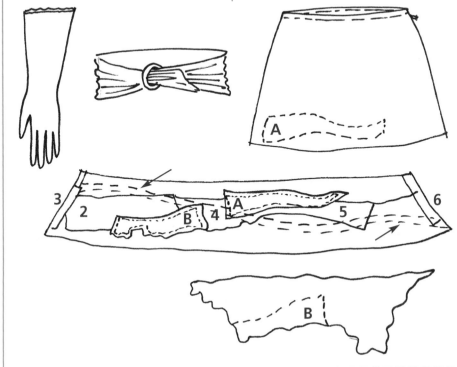

4. With right side up, thread ends of ribbon though topmost belt loop sections, as shown.

Place belt around waist, with opening in front. Cross ribbons in an X shape, and thread ends through opposite bottommost belt loop sections, just like lacing a shoe, as shown.

Wrap ribbons around body as many times as you like, going through belt loops each time. Tie ribbons at front waist in a double bow, as shown, to secure belt and echo an obi.

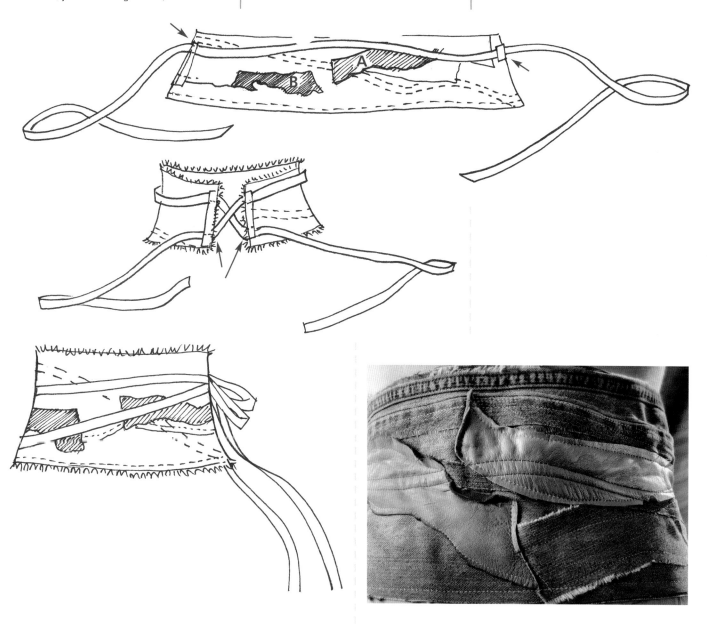

stitched headband

REQUIRED TIME:
30 MINUTES
(MUST USE A
SEWING MACHINE
ON THIS PROJECT)

Blue jeans suit different moods, whether it's wearing them to go to a bar or apple picking or driving the kids to grandmother's house. They harken back to the spirit of America, really.

— Mark-Evan Blackman, a former designer for Evan-Picone and chairman of the menswear design department at the Fashion Institute of Technology

All hair types work with this simple headband—afro, wavy, straight, curly, braided, and locs. It can be worn day or night and adds an instant splash of fun to your ensemble. Finish with any of the techniques from pages 12–15. The elastic back makes it easy to wear and, as it only requires a small piece of denim, it can easily and quickly be jazzed up or left simple for a more timeless, trend-free look. So tame your wild and woolly bangs or prevent unwanted tendrils from hanging in your face with this dynamic bandeau.

Materials

STANDARD MATERIALS

Scissors

Marking devices

Aleene's Fabric Glue

Seam ripper

Heavy-duty straight pins

Measuring devices

Embroidery scissors

Sewing machine and sewing machine needles

Thread in matching or contrasting colors

Iron and ironing board

SPECIAL MATERIALS

1 pair of jeans, any size—we suggest dark denim
for this project

1¼-inch-wide elastic, 4 inches long

Scrap of contrasting fabric (of any kind), at least 2
by 8 inches

1. Lay jeans flat, right side up, with front facing up. Mark cutting lines for pieces A–D, as shown below. Pieces A–C (appliqués) can be any dimension and shape; piece D (headband base) should be at least 17 inches long and 4 inches wide.

NOTE: If you want to use a zipper placket or pockets, you must remove zipper (see page 47, Step 6) and deconstruct extra denim layers (see page 37).

Using scissors, cut out all pieces along cutting lines, through 1 layer only.

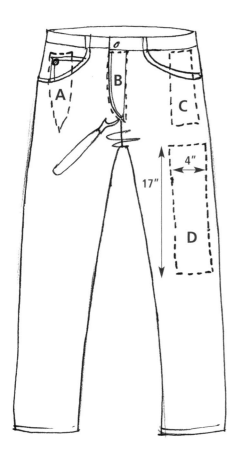

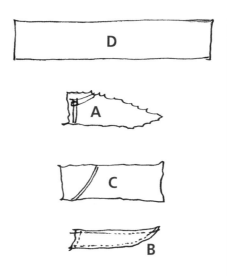

2. Lay headband base D flat, with right side facing up. Place appliqué pieces A-C, right side up, on headband, arranging pieces as you desire. Using fabric glue, glue appliqués in place (see page 34). When glue is dry, topstitch appliqués to headband, ⅛ inch from raw edges, through all layers.

3. Turn headband over so wrong side is facing up. Fold back each end of headband ½ inch, as shown, then stitch close to raw edge, through all layers, as shown.

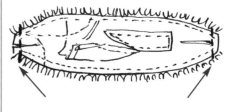

4. From contrasting fabric, cut a piece about 2 inches wide by 8 inches long.

Lay contrasting fabric flat with *wrong* side facing up. Place elastic, horizontally, at lower right-hand corner of fabric, as shown. Fold fabric lengthwise, over elastic. Pin, then stitch one end, through elastic and both layers of fabric to secure, as shown. Right side of fabric is now showing.

Pull loose end of elastic through to unsewn end of folded fabric, and pin. (Note: Elastic is half the length of fabric, so fabric will pucker when you do this.)

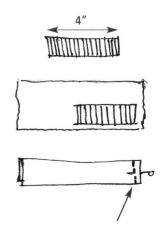

5. Place fabric with elastic inside under presser foot of sewing machine. Stitch across pinned end, then pivot at corner and, pulling elastic taut as you stitch so fabric lies flat, stitch long sides of fabric together, ¼ inch from raw edges, as shown. Do NOT sew elastic into this seam; elastic is sewn into seams at each *end* of piece, not on the long side. When you remove this piece from machine, it will be gathered up, as shown in detail. (If you have a zigzag stitch on your machine you can use that.)

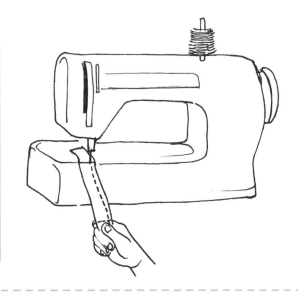

detail of gathered elastic

6. Lay headband flat, *wrong* side up. Place 1 end of fabric-covered elastic over 1 end of headband, overlapping by ½ inch; stitch, as shown below. Do the same with the other side, attaching elastic to headband. (All seam allowances are on wrong side of headband.)

When you wear headband, elastic goes at back of neck, under hair.

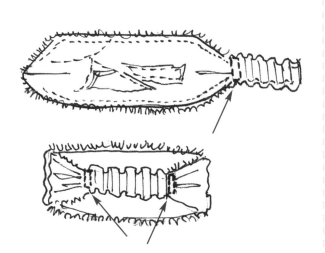

legwarmers

REQUIRED TIME:
40 MINUTES
(MUST USE A
SEWING MACHINE
ON THIS PROJECT)

These combo knit and denim legwarmers are made from the pocket part of a pair of jeans sewn to a sweater sleeve. Unexpectedly offbeat, quirky, and expressive, this is a classic Sistahs style choice. Though these legwarmers fit right on top of any pants, we think they look best on top of your jeans. It's a double-whammy look: A denim-on-top-of-denim style.

Wouri Vice, celebrity stylist, is always searching for the next big thing. With the trend cycle getting shorter by the minute, Wouri spotted our legwarmers while pulling sample shirts for Alicia Keys. He stopped in his tracks, glanced at us, and shouted, "I've seen legwarmers, but these are legwarmers for the stars!"

We always feel elated when people connect with our clothing. It's similar to the first day of high school, college, or a new job. You want those around you to understand your vision and your point of reference. It's about sharing your journal while others critique. Some will like it. Others will not.

Materials

STANDARD MATERIALS

Scissors

Marking devices

Aleene's Fabric Glue

Seam ripper

Heavy-duty straight pins

Measuring devices

Sewing machine and sewing machine needles

Thread in matching or contrasting colors

Iron and ironing board

SPECIAL MATERIALS

1 pair of fairly worn, boot-cut jeans in a very small size, depending on how large your calf muscles are

Firmly knitted sweater (like the jacquard used here) with cuffs

1. Lay jeans flat, right side up, with front facing up. Mark horizontal cutting lines across legs, 19 inches down from waistband, as shown.

Mark one vertical cutting line down inside of one leg from waistband, just inside zipper placket, crotch seam, and inside of leg seam, as shown below. Mark a second vertical cutting line down inside of other leg as shown, starting below zipper placket.

Turn jeans over so back of jeans are facing up. Mark vertical cutting lines from waistband, down 19 inches, and going through middle of pockets, as shown. Then mark horizontal cutting lines, 19 inches down from waistband, matching horizontal lines on jeans front.

Using scissors, carefully cut along all cutting lines. Be sure to cut through only 1 layer of jeans, as cutting lines on back and front are different. Do NOT cut along side seams; leave them intact. Your pieces will be about 1 to 1½ inches wider at the bottom than they are at the top, as shown below.

On piece A with the zipper, remove zipper from zipper placket (see page 47, step 6). Trim away crotch triangle, so finished cut piece looks as shown. Deconstruct extra denim layers from top 1 inch of pockets (see page 37).

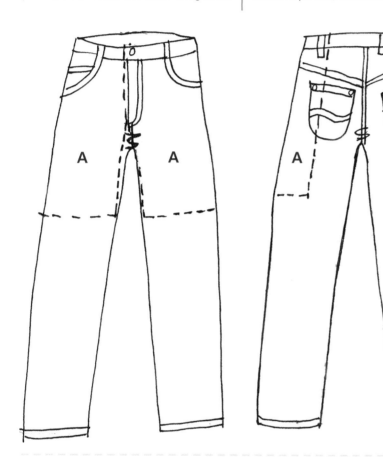

2. Lay sweater flat, right side out and front facing up. Cut off 19 inches of each sleeve, as shown. Then, cut off inside sleeve seam all the way to bottom of cuff, as shown. (Note that the pieces cut from the sweater should be exactly the same dimensions as the pieces cut from the jeans in step 1. If not, trim as neccessary.)

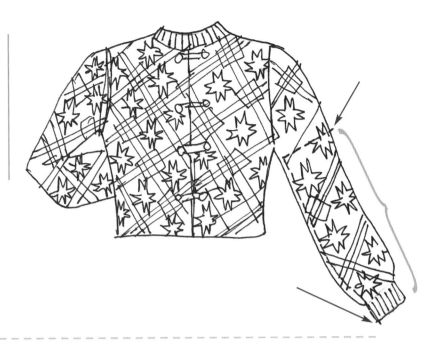

3. Lay denim pieces flat with right sides facing up. Place sweater pieces facedown, with cuff at waistband over denim pieces, so *right* sides are facing. Using fabric glue, place glue along one long edge of sweater fabric (on *right* side of sweater fabric), and glue sweater fabric to jeans fabric (see page 34).

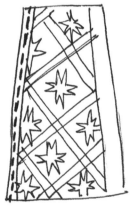

4. When glue is dry, stitch ¹/₂-inch seams. Turn pieces right side out and topstitch ¹/₈ inch from seam, as shown. Repeat process for remaining seams on both legwarmers.

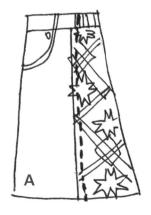
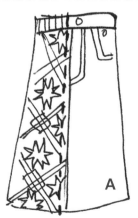

glossary

ACCENT - emphasis or prominence given to a line or decorative color in costume

A-LINE - slightly flared from the waist or shoulders

APPLIQUÉ - decoration laid and applied to another surface; ornamentation applied to a piece of material

AWL - a pointed tool used for making holes in leather and fabric

BACKSTITCH - an overlapping stitch made by starting next stitch at middle of preceding one; used for strength in plain sewing and embroidery

BASTE - to make a series of long, widely spaced straight stitches by hand or machine to temporarily hold two or more layers of fabric together or to mark a stitching line; also used for gathering fabric

BIAS - the direction of a piece of woven fabric, usually referred to simply as "the bias"; bias runs at 45° angle to its warp (straight grain line) and weft (cross grain line) threads.

BIAS TAPE - a narrow strip of fabric, cut on the bias, used in piping, binding seams, finishing raw edges, and as decorative detail; varies in width from ½ inch to 3 inches. The bias cut gives bias tape four-way stretch, and makes it more fluid and easier to drape than a fabric strip that is cut on the straight or cross grain lines. Bias cuts lay smoothly across curves and straight edges alike. Many strips can be pieced together into a long "tape."

BODICE - the torso part of a shirt or dress that extends from the waist to the shoulder and around the body

BOBBIN - a thread holder that feeds the bottom thread in machine sewing. Housed in a bobbin case, it lies directly under the metal plate beneath the sewing foot that holds the fabric in place while you sew.

CARE LABEL - a required label in which manufacturers and importers provide at least one satisfactory method of care necessary for the ordinary use of the garment. Most labels include fabric, content, cleaning, and ironing instructions, and the region where the garment was made.

CENTER BACK FOLD (C.B.F.) - the exact (vertical) middle line on the back of a garment or garment part. To determine C.B.F., fold the garment in half lengthwise, with the back side facing up; the fold line is the C.B.F.

CENTER FRONT FOLD (C.F.F.) - the exact (vertical) middle line on the front of a garment or garment part. To determine C.F.F., fold the garment in half lengthwise, with the front side facing up; the fold line is the C.F.F.

CLEAN SEAM - a seam stitched and pressed open; it looks invisible, from a distance; when viewed closely, it looks like a straight line.

COUTURE - a French word meaning "sewing" or "needlework"; the business of designing, making, and selling highly fashionable, usually custom-made clothing for women; the high-fashion clothing created by designers

CUMMERBUND - a broad, fitted sash that fits around the waist, generally pleated

CUT - the style and manner in which a garment is cut and made; the fit of a garment; to make or fashion by cutting

CUTTING LINE (CUTTING PATH) - a line that you follow when cutting out garment and other fabric pieces

DECONSTRUCTION - taking apart an existing garment, accessory, etc., and transforming it into something else (e.g., an old tie becomes a belt, a T-shirt becomes a halter or skirt, a T-shirt becomes a skirt, etc.); when applied to seams, the removal of all but two outer fabric layers from various seams

DISAPPEARING INK MARKER - a marking device used on fabric that completely vanishes after a certain amount of time, with or without washing in cold water

DRAWSTRING - string, cording, rope, ribbon, etc., running through a fabric tunnel or channel, which when pulled draws the fabric into a tight gather

DRESSMAKER'S TRACING PAPER - tracing paper designed specifically for fabrics and sewing because the ink easily washes and/or irons out; used with a tracing wheel to mark and transfer cutting and sewing lines, design details, and other sewing guides to fabrics (or to paper patterns)

EMBELLISHMENTS - adornments, decorative items added to a garment for style appeal, such as sequins, jewels, trims, appliqués, etc.

EMPIRE WAIST - a high waist, above the waistline, at or just under the bust line

EYELET - a small hole or perforation usually rimmed with metal, cord, fabric, or leather; used to reinforce a hole; can be decorative or functional

FABRIC GLUE - an adhesive used specially for fabric that is long lasting through laundering and is not stiff when it dries

FASTENER - device that fastens or holds together separate fabric parts, such as buttons, snaps, and hooks and eyes

FINDINGS - the thread, tapes, trims, buttons, seam or bias binding, hooks and eyes, zippers or slide fasteners, and other sewing essentials used in garment making

FRAY - to wear away (the edges of fabric, for example) by rubbing; a threadbare spot, as on fabric.

GRAIN - direction the threads in fabric run. Straight grain is the long grain running parallel to the selvage and has little or no stretch; the cross grain runs perpendicular to the straight grain and selvage, and has a fair amount of stretch. The bias (running at a 45° angle to straight and cross grains) provides the most stretch.

GROMMET - a metal eyelet, inserted into cloth or leather, through which a fastener may be passed

HAND – the texture or feel of the fabric/cloth (e.g., the softness, coarseness, pliability, etc.)

HANDSEWING NEEDLES – needles that come sized, in various lengths and thicknesses; different sizes work with different types of fabrics. Handsewing needles are named according to their purpose, such as: sharps, betweens, ballpoint, embroidery, leather, beading, chenille, upholstery, darning, and tapestry.

HAND SANDING – a way of reproducing wear and tear, such as whiskers, chevrons, or other damage marks in localized areas on newer fabrics, simulating long-term wear

HARDWARE – metal goods such as buckles, studs, grommets, etc.

HEM – the fabric at the bottom of a garment or sleeve that is folded to the wrong side (skirt, pant, and dress hems are usually 2 inches; sleeve hems, 1 to 1½ inches)

HEMLINE – the finished length of a garment or sleeve; the line where you fold the fabric to the wrong side to make the hem

HEM GAUGE – a device used for measuring and turning hems in one step

HOOK AND EYE – a type of fastener in two pieces—a hook and a loop—which link together to secure the openings on garments

ILLUSTRATION – graphics, e.g., pictures, drawings, etc., that help to make something clear

INSEAM – the inner leg seam of pants that runs from the crotch to the hem

INTERFACING – a moderately stiff/firm material used between layers of fabric to reinforce the fabric; often used in collars, lapels, cuffs, button and zipper plackets, and on the bodice of jackets.

IRON – a metal appliance with a handle and a weighted flat bottom; when heated, used to press wrinkles from fabric

IRONING BOARD – a long, narrow padded board, often with collapsible supporting legs, used as a working surface for ironing

IRON-ON HEM TAPE – a ½-inch-wide strip that is fusible on both sides so when you sandwich it between two fabric layers and apply dry heat, you fuse those two layers together

KIMONO – a garment typical of Japanese culture; a loose, wide-sleeved robe fastened around waist with broad sash

KIMONO SLEEVE – grandiose bell sleeve similar to sleeves on a *furisode* (a long-sleeved kimono)

MARK – to draw on fabric with tailor's chalk, pen or pencil, or with dressmaker's tracing paper, illustrating where the fabric is going to be cut or stitched; also indicates measurements and waist, bust, hip, and center lines

MEASURE – the act of measuring body parts, fabric pieces, and construction details; to mark, lay out, or establish dimensions by measuring

MONOCHROMATIC – containing or using one color scheme (for example: different shades of the same color (burgundy/red/fuchsia/pink/pastel pink)

NOTCH – an indentation or incision on an edge, used to indicate where to cut, sew, or fold fabric

PAILLETTES – similar to sequins but larger; used to embellish and adorn garments

PATCHWORK – varied colored patches of material sewn together, as in a quilt

PATTERN DRAFTING RULER (A.K.A. QUILTER'S RULER) – a wide, transparent plastic ruler often used for pattern drafting and marking fabric

PIN – noun: a small, slender piece of short wire with a head and a sharp point; verb: to join fabric layers together by running a pin in and out through fabric layers

PINK – to trim edge or cut with pinking shears

PINKING SHEARS – scissors with notched blades; used to finish cut edges with a zigzag cut for decoration or to prevent raveling or fraying

PRESS – to use a hot iron with plenty of steam to flatten open seams and stitching, and to remove wrinkles from fabrics; the key to easier sewing and fabulous tailoring (use "cotton" or highest heat setting for pressing denim)

RAW EDGE – unfinished seam or edge of fabric

RIBBING – raised rows of fabric arranged vertically or horizontally

RUFFLES – a strip of frilled or closely gathered fabric used for trimming or decoration

RUCHE – a ruffle or pleat of lace, muslin, or other light fabric used for trimming women's garments

SELVAGE – the reinforced long edge of a bolt of fabric, which is woven so that it will not unravel; this durable edging is desirable when making couture jeans

SASH – ornamental band, scarf, strip, or belt worn around the waist, hips, or over the shoulders

SCISSORS – sharp, long-bladed implement designed to cut fabric

SEAM – the joining line where parts of a garment are sewn together

SEAM ALLOWANCE – the distance between the seam line (stitching line) that joins two or more pieces of fabric together and the cut edge of the fabric

SEAM RIPPER – a small device with a small, sharp hook used to remove stitches from any seam

SECURE STITCH – backstitches used to secure hand or machine stitching; alternative to knotting threads

SILHOUETTE – the shape or outline of the natural body; the shape or outline of the garment

STITCH – a single turn or loop of the yarn or thread, in hand or machine sewing

STITCHING LINE – the actual line that you stitch (sew) on

SAFETY PIN – a pin in the form of a clasp that covers and holds the pin point in place; joins fabric layers more securely than straight pins

STRAIGHT PIN – a short, straight stiff piece of metal with a pointed end; used to fasten layers of cloth together before stitching

STYLE – the particular cut or design of a garment

TAILOR'S CHALK – comes in clay, wax, or crayon forms; used for marking on fabric to indicate cutting line, measurements, etc. (clay brushes out of fabric, whereas wax and crayon melt off with a hot, dry iron)

TAPE MEASURE – a length of cloth or plastic tape, 60 inches long, marked at ⅛-inch intervals; flexible tape hugs body curves when measuring

THREAD - a slender cord of varying degrees of fineness, produced by twisting together two or more filaments; spun from cotton, flax, silk, nylon, or other fibers

TRACING PAPER - semi-transparent paper used for tracing and transferring designs, shapes, etc. to fabrics and garment pieces

TRACING WHEEL - a small, toothed wheel with a handle (sort of like a pizza cutter); used with dressmaker's tracing paper to mark and transfer cutting and sewing lines, design details, and other sewing guides to fabrics (or to paper patterns)

TRIM - noun: lace, ribbon, braid, fringe, etc., used to decorate or adorn a garment; verb: the act of applying trim to a garment

VELCRO™ - fabric hook-and-loop fasteners used for connecting layers of fabric, or as closures

WARP - threads running the length of a woven fabric, parallel to the selvage; also known as the lengthwise grain

WEFT - threads running perpendicular to warp threads of a woven fabric; also known as the cross grain

WEIGHTS - any small weight (from fabric weights to household items) used to hold fabric steady on cutting and marking surface so fabric doesn't move when it's cut, pinned, marked, etc.

WHIPSTITCH - a short, easy, hand stitch used to join two finished edges, where the stitches pass over the raw edges diagonally; not an invisible stitch—often decorative

WHISKERS - the flattering wrinkles around the crotch of the jeans.

ZIGZAG STITCH - a chain stitch made by inserting a needle at an angle and alternating from side to side; looks similar to inverted letter z

ZIPPER - a fastening device consisting of parallel rows of metal, plastic, or nylon teeth on adjacent edges of an opening that are interlocked by a sliding tab

ZIPPER FOOT - a sewing machine attachment used when sewing on a zipper

resources

FOR YOUR DENIM NEEDS

Local Salvation Army or Goodwill
Family or friend's closets
Your closet
Flea markets
Church secondhand sales
Swap parties with friends
Yard sales
Local vintage boutiques
www.ebay.com
www.denimexpress.com
www.lanebryant.charmingshoppes.com

RIBBONS AND TRIMS

www.mjtrim.com
www.FashionFabricOnline.com
www.DistinctiveFabric.com
www.GalaxyTrim.com
www.fabric.com
www.butts4u.com ($15 minimum)
www.cybertrim.com
www.ejoyce.com

BASIC SEWING SUPPLIES AND NOTIONS

www.JoAnn.com
www.SewTrue.com
www.michaels.com
www.pearlpaint.com
www.wardrobesupplies.com

EMBELLISHMENTS

www.mybedazzle.com
www.myembellishments.com
www.grovegear.com (for patches)
www.glitzonline.com

LEATHER SCRAPS

www.4hides.com
www.triggleather.com
www.brettunsvillage.com
www.twsleather.com
www.skinnyllama.com

WHERE TO FIND US

www.sistahsofharlem.com

credits

Photography—Derrick Gomez www.derrick-gomez.com
Hair—Dana Gibbs (www.danasloft.com)
Makeup—Shadé Boyewa-Osborne
Photo Assistant—Alex Wong
Gaffer—Nat Aguilar
Stylist Assistant—Samiayah Johnson

ACCESSORIES

Pure Accessories Showroom www.pureaccessories.com
Kimina Baylli www.baylli.com
Alexis Bittar www.alexisbittar.com
Anu Rock and Metal Jewelry
    www.myspace.com/anurockmetal
Kimi Wear www.kimiwear.com
All clothing by Sistahs of Harlem except for top on pg 79. Top is stylist's own.

MODELS

Mariel Koeo @ Major Model Management
    www.majormodelmanagement.com
Amanda @ Major Model Management
    www.majormodelmanagement.com
Amy (Freelance)
Nekesha @ Ikon Model Management
    www.ikonmodels.com
Amber @ Images Management
    www.imagesnyc.com

index